Hannaman & **Kretz**[inger]

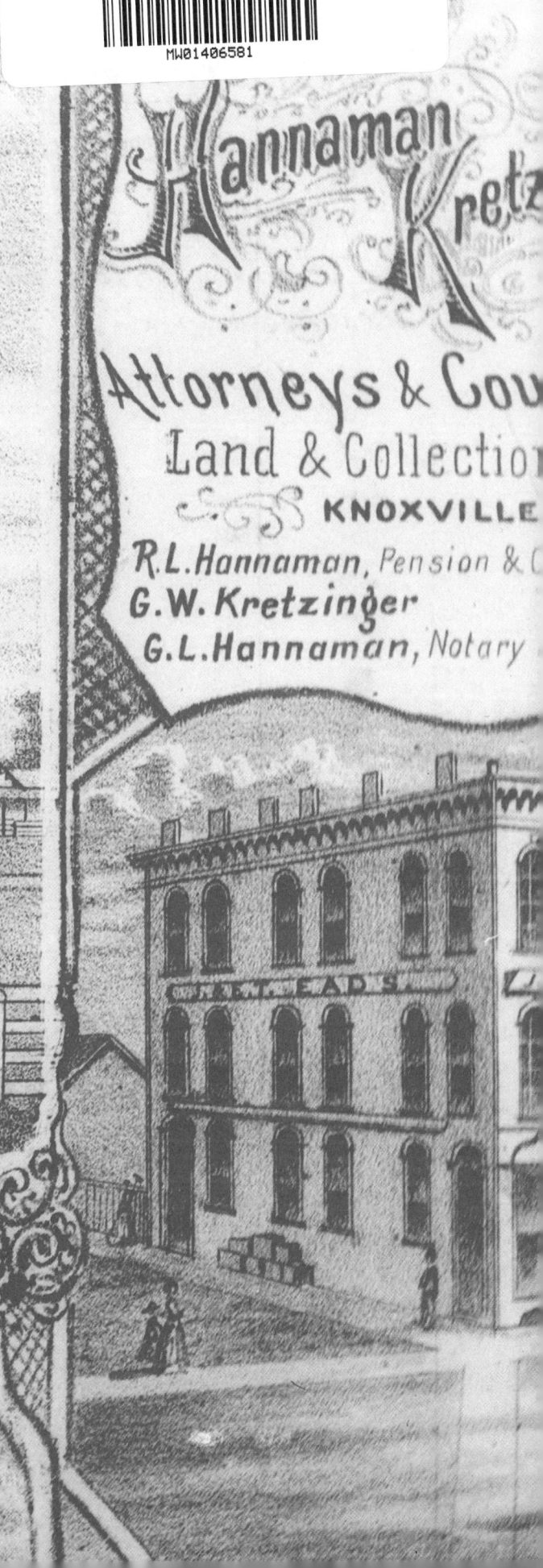

Attorneys & Cou[nselors]
Land & Collectio[n]
KNOXVILLE

R. L. Hannaman, Pension & C[laims]
G. W. Kretzinger
G. L. Hannaman, Notary

[K]NOXVILLE ILL. ILL-248

April 28, 2010

Richard,

A book you can enjoy continually as you peruse chapters at your leisure. The interesting history and beautiful pictures provide our type of reading.

Doug Hancock

Illinois Courthouses

An Illustrated History

As the sponsor for this publication, we dedicate this book to
William "Bill" John Anderson (1964-2008)
who gave more to increase interest in county government than most will ever know.

Sponsored by

Illinois Association of County Board Members
and Commissioners

Springfield, Illinois

This book is dedicated with love to Brooke, Zachary, Katherine, and Claire.

Copyright © 2009 by Dennis L. Weiser

All rights reserved, including the right to reproduce this work in any form whatsoever without permission in writing from the publisher, except for brief passages in connection with a review. For information, please write:

The Donning Company Publishers
184 Business Park Drive, Suite 206
Virginia Beach, VA 23462

Steve Mull, General Manager
Barbara Buchanan, Office Manager
Anne Cordray, Editor
Nathan Stufflebean, Graphic Designer
G. Bradley Martin, Project Director

Derek Eley, Imaging Artist
Debby Dowell, Project Research Coordinator
Tonya Hannink, Marketing Specialist
Pamela Engelhard, Marketing Advisor

Library of Congress Cataloging-in-Publication Data

Weiser, Dennis.
  Illinois courthouses : an illustrated history / Dennis Weiser.
     p. cm.
  ISBN 978-1-57864-601-2
  1. Courthouses--Illinois--Pictorial works. 2. Public buildings--Illinois--Pictorial works. 3. Public architecture--Illinois--Pictorial works. 4. Courthouses--Illinois--History. 5. Public buildings--Illinois--History. 6. Public architecture--Illinois--History. 7. Illinois--History, Local. 8. Counties--Illinois--History. 9. Illinois--Biography. I. Title.
  F542.W44 2009
  725.09773--dc22
                              2009041809
Printed in the United States of America by Walsworth Publishing Company

---

Dust jacket, front cover photo: McDonough County Courthouse
Dust jacket, back cover, top photo: Lincoln statue on the lawn of the old historic courthouse in Bloomington, Illinois (Sculptor: Rick Harney)
Dust jacket, back cover, bottom photo: Lincoln Draws the Line statue at Peoria, Illinois (Sculptor: John McLarey)
Dust jacket, back cover, background photo: Lincoln statue leaning on a split rail fence at Pontiac in Livingston County (Sculptor: Rick Harney)
Photo on opposite page: Pike County Courthouse
Photos on the Table of Contents (left to right):
1) An 1816 surveyor's field book and case kept in the archives at Henderson County Courthouse. Survey points and distances were noted in the surveyor's field book as he measured the land that would eventually become a town.
2) An 1809 map of the Illinois Territory as it appeared when it was created out of the Northwest Territory. It included the states of Illinois and Wisconsin and portions of Minnesota and Michigan. Kaskaskin (more common spelling is Kaskaskia) was the territorial capital. Illinois was admitted into the Union as a state in 1818.
3) An 1855 advertisement. A law office in Mercer County offered to assist veterans of the War of 1812 who wished to file a claim for free land in the Military Tract. The federal government had promised them acreage as "bounty" for their service in that war.
4) A railroad ticket issued in 1857 by Central Illinois Railroad. The Iron Horse reduced travel time between cities from weeks to days. By the 1850s the railroads were the dominate passenger and freight transportation service in Illinois. The Central Illinois became the largest railroad line in the world and connected Chicago with cities throughout the nation.
5) The Black Hawk or Eternal Indian statue is a 1908 sculpture by Lorado Taft that stands in the Lowden State Park near the city of Oregon, Illinois. The 48-foot tall, concrete monolithic statue overlooks the Rock River Valley. Black Hawk's band resisted with force the cession of land to settlers but signed a treaty surrendering their claim in 1833 opening the way for expansion and settlement of northern Illinois.
6) A plaque at the McDonough County Courthouse is symbolic of the connection that citizens throughout Illinois felt they had between themselves and the martyred president. Many courthouses maintain collections of his legal papers, statues, and other monuments to commemorate Lincoln's time in Illinois.

Illinois Courthouses

An Illustrated History

Dennis Weiser

Table of Contents

Foreword 6	Cook 34	State Capitals of Illinois 58
Preface 7	The Great Chicago Fire 36	Hancock 62
Introduction 8	Crawford 37	Hardin 63
Adams 14	Cumberland 38	Henderson 64
Alexander 16	DeKalb 39	Henry 65
U.S. Custom House at Cairo ... 17	DeWitt 40	Iroquois 66
Bond 18	Douglas 41	Jackson 68
Boone 20	DuPage 42	Jasper 69
Brown 21	Edgar 44	Jefferson 70
Bureau 22	Edwards 46	Jersey 72
Calhoun 23	Effingham 48	Jo Daviess 73
Carroll 24	Fayette 49	Johnson 74
Cass 25	Ford 50	Temple Burned, Temple Rebuilt ... 75
Champaign 26	Franklin 51	Kane 78
Christian 28	Fulton 52	Kankakee 80
Clark 30	Gallatin 53	Kendall 81
Clay 31	Greene 54	Knox 82
Clinton 32	Grundy 56	Lake 83
Coles 33	Hamilton 57	LaSalle 84

Lawrence 86	Morgan.. 114	St. Clair... 138
Lee 88	Moultrie 115	Stark... 140
Livingston 89	Ogle 116	Stephenson 141
Logan 90	Peoria 117	Tazewell 142
Macon 91	Perry 118	Union 144
Macoupin 92	Piatt 120	Vermilion 145
Madison 94	Pike 121	Wabash 146
Marion 96	Pope 122	Warren 148
Marshall 98	Pulaski 123	Washington 149
Mason 99	Putnam 124	Wayne 150
Massac 100	The Plow that Opened the Prairie. 125	White 151
McDonough 102	Randolph 126	Whiteside 152
McHenry 103	Richland 128	Will 153
McLean 104	Rock Island 130	Williamson 154
Menard 105	Saline 131	Winnebago 155
Lincoln, the Courthouse Lawyer.. 106	Sangamon 132	Woodford 156
Mercer 110	Schuyler 134	Measuring Architectural .... 158 Treasures: Courthouses and the Historic American Buildings Survey (HABS)
Monroe 111	Scott 136	
Montgomery 112	Shelby 137	About the Author 160

Foreword

A courthouse, American novelist William Faulkner said in his 1951 *Requiem for a Nun*, is "the center, the focus, the hub; sitting looming in the center of the county's circumference like a single cloud in its ring of horizon, laying its vast shadow to the utmost rim of horizon; musing, brooding, symbolic and ponderable, tall as cloud, solid as rock, dominating all: protector of the weak, judicate and curb of the passions and lusts, repository and guardian of the aspirations and the hopes."

Illinois has long been connected with some of the most important names in architecture, from the prairie style homes pioneered by Frank Lloyd Wright to Daniel Burnham's famous skyscrapers lining the Chicago River. Buildings reflect time and vision. County courthouses are arguably some of the most intriguing.

Courthouses are part of American life—symbols of justice and independence. Similar to family heirlooms, these architectural treasures convey the spirit and leadership of the citizenry that built them.

I am fortunate to have a job that requires me to travel Illinois. On my long drives through the state, I have walked many public squares to take in the strength and beauty emanating from these wondrous buildings. In many towns, the courthouse is the most visible structure with a handcrafted cupola or stately clock tower piercing the sky. The brick or stone structures boast a rich heritage of exterior architectural design, often complimented by humble memorials on the lawn that bear eloquent witness to the lives of previous generations.

In *Illinois Courthouses: An Illustrated History*, photojournalist Dennis Weiser has skillfully woven this valuable original material into a compelling narrative, creating a truly phenomenal oral and photographic history of the courthouses in Illinois. Within these pages the author has captured well the flavor of time and economic circumstances which provoked the building of these public structures.

Over the years, Illinois' courthouses have seen proud times, troublesome times, and tragic times. Today these historic buildings stand as centerpieces of the community—where the past is still a presence. This is not just a book to read; it is a tribute to the competence of the people of Illinois. It is a book to cherish, and to give.

Kelly J. Murray
Executive Director
Illinois Association of County Board Members
and Commissioners

Preface

It is obvious that most nineteenth and early twentieth century courthouses were relatively modest building projects as compared to public building construction and remodeling that has taken place in more recent years. These frugal historic buildings nevertheless are excellent structures and architecturally significant. When the need to replace or renovate occurs, one can only hope that preservation and restoration will be the first choice of action. To establish a consistent comparison between the cost of construction of historic courthouses and modern dollar amounts, the author consulted Samuel H. Williamson's "Six Ways to Compute the Relative Value of a U.S. Dollar Amount, 1790 to Present."

The photographs in this volume are by the author unless otherwise noted. The artwork, statues, monuments, and photographs of courthouses no longer in existence shown herein are pieces in the collections of the various courthouses represented and the artist is identified whenever possible. However, some artwork was put in place by itinerant journeyman artists whose work was unsigned. Many of the historic photographs, maps, and illustrations included in the book are from the digital files of the Library of Congress, Historic American Buildings Survey / Historic American Engineering Record and are so noted.

The author appreciates the information provided to him during visits to the courthouses, local museums, libraries, and information provided by genealogical and historical society web sites and publications, Chambers of Commerce and tourism guides, centennial and sesquicentennial celebration programs, Illinois Secretary of State historic archives, county records and minutes, historic newspaper articles, and the ubiquitous county histories circa 1880s, published by Brink, McDonough & Company of Philadelphia; Charles C. Chapman & Company, Chicago; and others.

Special thanks to the Cairo Public Library and Monica L. Smith, Deere & Company, Sheriff John H. Monnet, Deputy Sheriff Ken Oakley, Associate Judge Steven R. Bordner, Iroquois County Historical Society and Ginny Lee, Jackson County Treasurer Shirley D. Booker, McLean County Museum of History and Greg Koos, Circuit Court Administrative Assistant Kay Batz, Schuyler County Treasurer Dean Ross, Circuit Judge Alesia A. McMillen, Circuit Judge Stephen D. White, and Circuit Court Administrative Assistant Arvella Guidotti. Thanks also to the men and women working in county government and those who provide security for these buildings on a daily basis.

President Thomas Jefferson helped introduce the neoclassical architectural style in America. His design for the 1822 University of Virginia rotunda is considered a seminal work that inspired state and federal building design over the next fifty years. (Library of Congress, Prints and Photographs Division, Historic American Buildings Survey)

8 | Illinois Courthouses

Introduction

Illinois has an interesting collection of courthouses that have been constructed in a variety of historic architectural styles. Nearly 70 percent of the courthouses currently in service around the state were constructed before 1920. Those courthouses serve as architectural time capsules, preserving design elements that prevailed during the mid-1800s and up to the early 1920s. These buildings exhibit architectural elements from across the spectrum of the complex neoclassical mode: Greek Revival (temple front) Romanesque, French, Italianate—all popular styles during the nineteenth century, and the Second Renaissance Revival period: classically influenced structures, but minus the towers, turrets, arches, and heavy stone work—a compromise approach that was favored from about 1900 to the Great Depression.

Unfortunately, there are no examples of courthouses built in the hewn-log or foursquare fashion that was common during the state's early nineteenth century expansion and development. Thankfully, there are photographs, paintings, and drawings to illustrate those styles. The courthouses built during the Great Depression and postwar eras are included in this history, too. They are noteworthy in their own right as they demonstrate current architectural trends that stress operational economy and efficiency.

The high-water mark in the construction of ornate Illinois courthouses was reached during the 1880s and 1890s when twenty-eight of the current courthouses were built. The number dropped to ten in the 1900s and nine in the 1910s. There were two in the 1920s. Fifty-six of the current 102 county courthouses were constructed in this time frame.

These courthouses were designed by a variety of architects. Joseph Royer was the most prolific with seven of the buildings to his credit: Grundy (1912), Clay (1912), Douglas (1911), Marion (1910), Ford (1905), Piatt (1903), and Champaign (1899) counties. Elijah Myers, who designed the Macoupin County and McDonough County courthouses, was perhaps the most famous—he being the only architect in America to design three different state's capitols: Michigan (1872), Texas (1885), and Colorado (1889). The output of all of the architects working in Illinois during this period can be lumped under the heading of "neoclassical."

That style—with elements drawn from a broad array of Roman and Greek influences—had been introduced in America by an amateur architect by the name of Thomas Jefferson. Jefferson used the Greek Revival (temple form) when he designed buildings for the University of Virginia and the style soon became the standard for state and federal buildings. The movement reflected America's desire to connect its democratic experiment with the classical Roman and Greek empires. In the public eye, columns, pediments, domes, porticos, arches, and other elements of architectural design connected county government to the history and traditions of antiquity.

Some of the Illinois courthouses are dramatic examples of the movement, such as the 1868 Macoupin County and the 1872 McDonough County courthouses. The "million dollar" Macoupin County Courthouse, considered to be the most costly nineteenth-century courthouse built in Illinois, is a neoclassical gem. When it was finished, its temple-front portico, Joliet limestone façade, and classic Corinthian capitals surpassed the state capitol in grandeur, not to mention square footage. The McDonough County Courthouse is a less exuberant building, but its segmented bell tower, raised entrance, and quoins fit together in such a way as to denote civilization, order, and authority.

The introduction of the Second Renaissance Revival architectural style in courthouse building design represented a new direction in thinking about courthouse construction. The style emerged in Illinois around the beginning of the twentieth century and continued until the onset of the Great Depression in the 1930s. Its roots were planted during the Columbian Exposition, the 1893 world's fair that was held in Chicago, when the fair's architects re-emphasized the classical designs of the Greek and Roman buildings. The public's taste began to shift away from the gaudy, over-decorated, and ponderous look of the public buildings that had been adorned with gothic towers, heavy arches, and decorative turrets during the latter-half of the nineteenth century.

Beginning with the dawn of the twentieth century, courthouse plans in Illinois featured light colors, smooth stone, ground level entrances, and flat roofs. The goal was to create courthouses with a no-nonsense look, with no money wasted on slate roofs, turrets, and domes.

The majestic dome atop the 1868 Macoupin County Courthouse is reminiscent of the Capitol in Washington, D.C., whose similar "wedding-cake" cast iron framed dome had been added in the early 1850s. (Library of Congress, Prints and Photographs Division, Historic American Buildings Survey)

The Second Renaissance Revival style is demonstrated very well in the 1906 Cook County Courthouse. The building was designed by Holabird & Roche and housed both the county court and city hall. (Postcard, author's collection)

The 1901 Lee County Courthouse, designed by Charles E. Brush, began the trend in Illinois. The 1903 DeKalb County Courthouse, designed by Watson & Hazleton, was inspired by Brush's Lee County Courthouse. The DeKalb County Courthouse's two-story colonnade, pediment with decorative sculpture, and composite capitals effectively combined the classical elements with the modern lines of a twentieth-century building. It was the first courthouse since the Civil War to be built without a dome or bell tower.

Not all courthouses are so clearly defined. Some of the nineteenth-century courthouses especially were less flamboyant; they relied on only a few architectural elements, such as a central dome, tower, or rusticated stone work to convey the neoclassical theme. A scarcity of decorative flourishes does not slight these courthouses. All are soundly built. The relative plainness, however, does make the point that few public buildings are "pure" throughout in their architectural design. The core of each building was constructed to be a workplace and its floor plan was drawn accordingly. A portico or tower defined the face of a structure but the obligation to provide office and court space dominated the shape of the body of the building. And, damage and modifications have caused some buildings to be altered in appearance over time. The 1895 Crawford County Courthouse, which lost its central tower due to a fire in 1899, is an example of this phenomenon.

Budgets were also a consideration. Construction of the first courthouse in a county was usually financed by selling parcels of public land or paid for by the corporation that founded the town in exchange for being named as the county seat. That was sufficient for a log or frame building, but in following years when communities were ready to build a larger and more

The commemorative column dedicated to the war dead of Peoria County was erected on the courthouse lawn in 1866. It represents the many similar monuments to be found at courthouses throughout the state.

12 | Illinois Courthouses

Left: Lincoln and Douglas met at Ottawa to debate the issue of expanding slavery into new territories. The abolition of slavery was a plank in Lincoln's newly formed Republican Party and Douglas, a Democrat, argued in favor of the decision being made by the state instead of at the federal level. The statues of Lincoln and Douglas were created by artist Rebecca Childers Caleel and were installed in 2002.

Right: The appellate courthouse at Ottawa was built in 1857 to house meetings of the Illinois Supreme Court but was commissioned as an appellate court in the 1870s. An excellent example of architectural harmony, the building is a prized example of the Classical Revival style—despite a shadowy reputation gained during the Civil War years.

elaborate structure, the money had to be raised by taxing the citizens. Sometimes the voters were agreeable and sometimes not so much. Some county officers grew weary of seeking public approval and circumvented the will of the people by "remodeling" the old courthouse to its foundations and building anew. That tactic worked in a few cases, but it always left a bad taste with the residents who eventually had to bite the bullet and pay for the subterfuge. Politicians learned that frugality in planning and design helped insure passage of a bond issue to build a new courthouse, but, even in the tightest of times, the public had a firm idea about what a courthouse should look like and they expected a touch of architectural excitement for their money.

In addition to reflecting the community's collective verdict about design, a courthouse influences citizens in other ways, too. In the years before radio, television, and the Internet, courtrooms and courthouse lawns were the "stage" for public discourse about national events. Washington Square in Ottawa, the county seat of LaSalle County, was the scene of the first Lincoln-Douglas debates of 1858. The historic debate attracted more than ten thousand people that hot afternoon of August 21.

In some cases, the debates in and around the courthouse were not so noble. The appellate courthouse that also stands on the northeast corner of Washington Park, a stone's throw from the debate site, was alleged to be a meeting place for the Knights of the Golden Circle a few months later. The Knights were members of a "copperhead" group that favored the Confederate cause.

Without question, a courthouse is the county's hall of justice. The purpose of the building is to deliver county services and see that the law is administered fairly and impartially. But, visitors are remiss if they do not take a moment to also acknowledge that the busy place of justice also hallows the county's fallen soldiers and champions. The stone and bronze statues on courthouse lawns instruct generations of children about the sacrifices made by gallant men and women who ventured into the larger world to support a noble cause, even at the greatest cost possible.

An Illustrated History | 13

Adams County

Organized: January 13, 1825

County Seat: Quincy

Named for: John Quincy Adams

Left: The 1950 courthouse was designed by the firm of Holabird, Root and Burgee. Supervising architects were Hafner and Hafner. The architectural firm of Poepping, Stone and Bach Associates supervised a 1994 remodel.

In 1818, John Wood, a young man still in his twenties, purchased 160 acres for $60 (about $1,200 in 2007). The land was located in the remote Military Track of western Illinois and part of Pike County. The "Track" was a reserve of thousands of acres of government land that had been set aside as bounty for veterans of the War of 1812, the brief naval war that America fought with England over impressing her sailors and which is best remembered because of Andrew Jackson's victory at the Battle of New Orleans. The war had ended three years earlier and Wood saw potential in the vast federal preserve.

Wood farmed his land diligently but his goal was to prosper from the development of the area rather than as a farmer. To attract more settlers to the region, he founded the town of Quincy and, in 1824, even as his new town was taking root, published a petition calling for Quincy and the surrounding area to be designated as Adams County. Wood evidently had good political connections. His request was quickly granted during the 1825 term of the General Assembly. (Wood was a lifelong accomplished politician, eventually serving as the mayor of Quincy, governor, and being appointed quartermaster general of the United States by Abraham Lincoln.)

Left: Architect J.S. McKean designed the 1875 courthouse.

Middle Left: The 1836 courthouse was a temple-front construction, a popular design of the day. In 1875, the building unfortunately was gutted by fire.

Bottom Left: Outside steps led to the second-story county offices in the 1826 hewn-log courthouse. Some courthouses of this style were built with the steps constructed inside the building and protected from the weather, but judges generally preferred that stairs to county offices be placed on an exterior wall to reduce foot traffic through the courtroom while court was in session.

Wood also was determined that Quincy would be named as the county seat even though it was situated on a bluff overlooking the Mississippi River and far from the geographic center of the new county. When the legislature's committee arrived in Quincy to search for a likely site to place the county seat, as was required by law, one of Wood's friends, Willard Keyes, "guided" the men into a bog where they spent the day slogging through mud up to their knees. The committee voted the next day to name Quincy as the county seat rather then schlep through the wilderness again.

The first courthouse was a hewn-log building erected in 1826. The second was a Classical-Revival style building. Constructed in 1836, that courthouse was destroyed by fire on January 9, 1875. A clogged flue caused the blaze.

The courthouse fire triggered a contest over the location of the county seat. Coatsburg, a town at the geographic center of the county, challenged Quincy for the honor but it was defeated in the general election of November 1875. Quincy remained the seat of justice.

The 1875 courthouse was destroyed on April 12, 1945, when a tornado churned its way across the Mississippi River, crowned the bluff, and plowed its way into Quincy's downtown section. Most of the buildings in the center of the town were destroyed along with the courthouse. The current courthouse was dedicated in 1950.

An Illustrated History | 15

Alexander County

Organized: March 4, 1819

County Seat: Cairo

Named for: State Senator William M. Alexander

Above Left: The current courthouse in Cairo was built in the 1960s.

Above Right: The Thebes 1846 courthouse could be seen from the valley below and is remembered as an impressive structure. White men came to Thebes to harvest the timber groves. The trees were lashed together and floated downriver to New Orleans. (Artist: J. Morgan)

Above: The Unity courthouse was burned by two escaping prisoners. The town was the county seat for only two years. The loss of the courthouse may have contributed to the county seat being moved so quickly.

Alexander County was the first county organized in the new state of Illinois by the legislature in December 1818. Governor Shadrach Bond made it official with his signature in March 1819. Cairo, located at the point where the Ohio River meets the Mississippi River, is the town highlighted on every map of the west during America's era of westward expansion. Fur traders, settlers, and soldiers knew it well as they traveled along the key western river routes of the nineteenth century. Cairo seemed the likely candidate to be named as the county seat.

Nevertheless, Alexander County bypassed its commercial and political center and selected the town of America to be the county seat between the years of 1819 and 1843. The honor shifted next to the town of Unity for a couple of years and then on to the town of Thebes in 1845. The area around Thebes was rich in timber and the trees were harvested to be floated downstream for sale at Natchez and the port of New Orleans. An historic courthouse was built there in 1846 on a bluff overlooking the river valley. It was designed by architect H. Ernst Barkhausen.

In 1859, the threat of civil war finally led to the selection of Cairo as the county seat. Because of its key location on the rivers' confluence, it assumed military significance in addition to its other attributes. Soon after the outbreak of hostilities, General U. S. Grant commandeered it as his headquarters for the Western Campaign. The county seat was a major supply depot and hospital center for the Union troops throughout the struggle between the north and south.

A classic courthouse was constructed at Cairo in 1865. The current courthouse was built almost one hundred years later, in the mid-1960s.

The 1865 Cairo courthouse served for nearly one hundred years. It was razed in 1963. The name "Cairo" was picked because of the town's supposed similarity to the Mediterranean port city of Cairo, Egypt. Thebes was named in similar fashion. (Artist: A. D. Johnston)

16 | Illinois Courthouses

U.S. Custom House at Cairo

In 1854, the U.S. Congress designated Cairo as Port of Delivery. A customs inspector boarded boats traveling upriver and collected fees on the goods that had passed the point of entry at New Orleans.

The federal government built a U.S. Custom House in 1867 to administer tariffs on those goods. Architect Alfred B. Mullett designed the building. The fireplaces were intended not for heat, but for ventilation. The interior wood is black and white walnut. Floors and hallways are white marble and black slate. Uprights in stairway banisters are iron with the railings of black walnut. All of the mail that was delivered to and from the west passed through this building, making the post office located on the first floor the third busiest station in the country.

Mullett also designed the San Francisco Mint, the U.S. Treasury Building and the old State Department Building in Washington, D.C. The Cairo Custom House is now a museum.

The Custom House has also served as a government office building—housing a post office, police headquarters, and weather bureau. At one time, the offices of the Alexander County circuit clerk and county treasurer were also located in this building. It was decommissioned as a government building in 1975 and converted into a museum during the 1980s.

Bond County

Organized: January 4, 1817

County seat: Greenville

Named for: Shadrach Bond, first Governor of Illinois

The 1884 courthouse in Greenville. The exterior has been returned to its original brick and stone finish.

In 1821, George Davidson, a land speculator and tavern owner, donated twenty acres to Bond County to be used as a county seat. The county set aside lots in the center of the property to serve as a public square and then auctioned the surrounding lots to raise money for building a courthouse, jail, and a pen to hold horses and cattle that strayed from their owners.

The 1884 courthouse was coated during the 1930s and 1940s with stucco and painted gray. The tower, shown in this photo, was removed in 1948.

In 1822, Robert G. White was hired to build a courthouse but, according to a critical record of his work, the use of inferior material and storm damage weakened the structure until it had to be razed and replaced in 1832. Eben Twiss built the second courthouse, a frame building, and it was replaced in 1853. Daniel W. Norris built the third courthouse. That building was destroyed by fire on March 24, 1883. A down-draft stirred the ashes in a fireplace and flying sparks ignited a blaze. Smoke from the fire was sighted and State Attorney W. A. Northcott quickly organized a bucket brigade. The firefighters kept the flames in check long enough for Circuit Clerk T. P. Morey to rescue the county's records from the burning building. Northcott went on to serve two terms as Illinois' lieutenant governor from 1897 to 1905.

The 1884 courthouse was erected at a cost of $20,000 (about $414,000 in 2007). Architect W. R. Parsons designed the building. A lightning strike damaged the building's tower in 1948 and that part of the structure had to be removed.

The 1853 courthouse. The small building near the fence served as an arsenal and jail.

An Illustrated History | 19

Boone County

Organized: March 4, 1837

County Seat: Belvidere

Named for: Daniel Boone

Left: The courthouse and the jail building were connected by a new bridge building during the 1980s restoration project. A new jail was built in 2003. There were steps near the entrance of the courthouse in 1870 "to aid old and infirm persons to get out of and into their vehicles."

Inset Above: General Stephan A. Hurlbut lived in Belvidere. In 1866 he became the first national commander of the Grand Army of the Republic. The GAR was founded at Decatur in Macon County. The group became a powerful national organization with more than 400,000 members. It was instrumental in securing many benefits for veterans and their survivors following the Civil War.

Boone County's initial court met on the morning of May 3, 1837, and the commissioners appointed officers for the first term. Boone County had been parceled from Winnebago County. Belvidere was an important stopping place on the Chicago-Galena stage route and developed as an agricultural trading center for shipping milk and grain to Chicago.

The town square and land upon which the courthouse stood was donated to the county by the Belvidere Company, a group of local investors. The agreement to donate the land stipulated that a courthouse be erected on that spot. The investors expected to profit from their generosity. Community development increased land values and altruism did not play a major role in the successful land speculation deals brokered in Illinois during the 1830s.

A county jail was constructed in April 1839, but the first courthouse building was not erected until 1843. The delay happened because the jail had to be torn down before the courthouse could be built. Too late, the county officials discovered the land upon which the jail had been built was actually the land that the Belvidere Company had intended as the site for the courthouse.

The county's courthouse, when it did get built, was a 40 by 30 foot, two-story building with a stone basement. The stone walls in the basement provided a secure jail and quarters for the sheriff. Family living space was also included on the first floor, along with the offices, and the second floor was used as a courtroom, community center, and meeting hall.

Construction on a replacement structure, the current courthouse, began in 1854 and was completed in 1855. This building is the second oldest courthouse in continuous service in the state.

Brown County

Organized: February 1, 1839

County Seat: Mount Sterling

Named for: Jacob Brown, General at the Battle of Sackett's Harbor

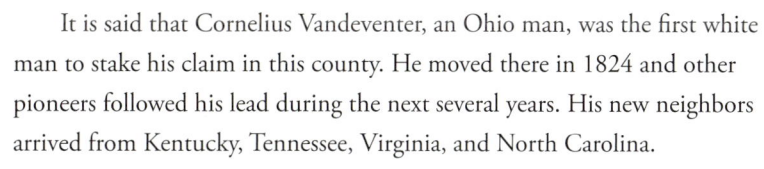

Top: The Brown County Courthouse was built in 1868 and destroyed by fire in 1939. The building was restored in 1942 under the supervision of architect Raymond G. Johnson.

Inset Left: An iconic photograph of Abraham Lincoln in his white suit is displayed on the courthouse wall at Mount Sterling. The photo was taken on May 7, 1858, shortly after Lincoln successfully defended Duff Armstrong in a murder trial at the courthouse in neighboring Cass County. Abe used the Old Farmer's Almanac *to show the jury that on the evening the crime was committed the moon was in its wane (dark) phase, proving that the prosecution's key witness lied about being able to see the crime "by the light of a full moon" as he claimed. (Photographer: Abraham Byers)*

Inset Right: Before being elected to the U.S. Senate, Stephen A. Douglas was a circuit court judge. He held court in Mount Sterling from 1841 to 1843. This daguerreotype of Douglas is notable because it shows the "Little Giant" in one of his less pugnacious poses. (Photographer: Calvin Kelsey)

It is said that Cornelius Vandeventer, an Ohio man, was the first white man to stake his claim in this county. He moved there in 1824 and other pioneers followed his lead during the next several years. His new neighbors arrived from Kentucky, Tennessee, Virginia, and North Carolina.

In 1829, Alexander Curry, a land speculator who thought the area had promise for further development, began buying parcels of unsettled land. Speculators were famous for creating new towns virtually overnight. They threw up a few rough buildings, marked right of ways and property lines in the dust, and then pronounced the site was a town. It did not always work but if enough settlers could be attracted to a developer's Potemkin village, the property blossomed into valuable real estate. The ones that failed to thrive disappeared like the Russian minister's picture-perfect towns that vanished once the Empress Catherine's barge had passed by.

Fortunately for Curry, he understood the three things that made property valuable: location, location, location. His settlement prospered and he named it Mount Sterling. In 1834, he had the town platted and subdivided into lots so that he could sell to businesses and tradesmen. At that time, Brown County still was part of Schuyler County.

In 1836, there was agitation to move Schuyler County's seat of justice from the town of Rushville, where it had been located since 1826, to a location closer to the center of the county. That effort failed, but the complaints from disgruntled voters alerted the Illinois legislature to the fact that Rushville was poorly situated to serve those residents living south of the La Moine River. In the spirit of never letting a crisis go to waste, in 1839 the General Assembly passed legislation to create Brown County and named Mount Sterling as the county seat. Rushville remained as the county seat for Schuyler County.

Mount Sterling prospered throughout the antebellum years as thousands of pioneers passed through the town on their way west. The town's main street also happened to be on the historic path that had been used for a millennium by Native Americans passing through the region and later the trail used by U.S. troops marching to the Mexican–American War of 1846 and then the '49ers headed for the California gold fields.

An Illustrated History | 21

Bureau County

Organized: February 28, 1837

County Seat: Princeton

Named for: Pierre de Bureo, the operator of a local trading post

The county commissioners authorized construction of Bureau County's first courthouse in 1837. They erected a frame building on the public square. The cost of the building was $7,500 ($152,000 in 2007). The building, as was common practice, served as the town's meeting hall when court was not in session.

In 1845, a second courthouse had to be built and the county issued bonds for $9,000 ($203,000 in 2007). The county selected brick as the building material. A wing was added to the structure in 1860. The addition cost $16,700 ($335,000 in 2007). The enlarged building served the county well until 1936.

In December 1935, when the country was at the deepest point of the Great Depression, the county authorities cautiously asked the voters to approve selling bonds to pay for courthouse improvements. They hoped only to secure enough funding to match a Federal Works Progress Administration (WPA) grant so they might enlarge and refurbish the old 1845 courthouse. The voters approved the bond issue and the county received word that their WPA grant check was in the mail. The twist was that the building committee decided instead to push ahead and construct an entirely new building. The expense must have been within the original parameters approved by the voters, however, because there seems to have been no outcry over the last minute switch.

The 1936 courthouse design is described in a publication issued by the Bureau County Architectural Preservation Society: "The linear hard edge style and angular composition of this Bedford limestone building characterizes the Art Deco style. The series of set back windows gives vertical emphasis to the façade. The octagonal lamps are common to this style. The building was constructed as a WPA project in a manner so as to convey the idea of authority or power."

At a time when the nation tottered on the verge of economic collapse and the number of unemployed was at 25 percent, the idea of authority and power was exactly what the building committee was shooting for.

The 1936 courthouse was designed by architectural firm of Royer & Danely. It is one of only six courthouses that were built in Illinois during the WPA (1936–1943) era.

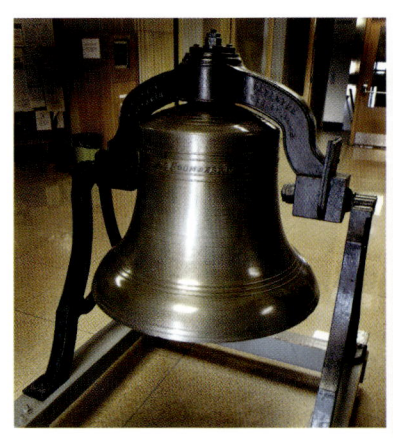

This clock bell hung in the 1845 courthouse.

22 | Illinois Courthouses

Calhoun County

Organized: January 10, 1825

County Seat: Hardin

Named for: John C. Calhoun, South Carolina Senator

Top: The Calhoun County Courthouse was extensively expanded in 1978. The architect for the remodeling project was V. Hanner and Associates.

Bottom: This view of the 1848 Hardin courthouse was made in 1903. At that point it was still a 36 by 30 foot, brick, two-story building. The contractor was William D. Hamilton. During the 1840s, a guard spent the night in the jail to prevent escape. For a night's work, a guard earned 50¢ (about $115 in 2007). The building pictured on the left is the jail.

John Shaw, one of the area's early influential grandees, picked the town of Coles' Grove as the site for Calhoun County's first county seat. Wealthy and politically powerful, Shaw donated eighty acres of land to the county and twelve lots at the center of the town's plat where he wanted the courthouse and jail to be erected. After Coles' Grove was formally selected as the seat of justice, he renamed it "Gilead," perhaps hoping that a biblical reference might add panache to his drab little settlement.

Shaw's plans fell into place nicely. A jail and a single-story log courthouse were quickly built at Gilead, fulfilling the General Assembly's minimum requirements for establishing a county seat. County officers had no offices, however, and they had to rent space in buildings around the square until 1830. Dissatisfaction about the county seat's location in general and complaints about the lack of space to conduct the county's business at the courthouse fell on deaf ears. Finally, the citizens' resolve stiffened enough that they contacted the legislature to request that the county seat be moved to a new location. Alarmed, Shaw and his county officials bestirred themselves to build a new courthouse, one that was large enough to handle all of the people's business.

Benjamin Mun won the contract to construct the larger courthouse. That brick building was occupied in 1832. It was destroyed by a fire in 1847, but fortunately the county records were saved. Minus a working courthouse once more, there was renewed interest in moving the county seat to a new location.

Realizing that Gilead would never be accepted as the people's choice, Shaw nominated the town of Hamburg as a "temporary" replacement county seat. He owned that town as well and he pressed an empty storeroom into service as a courtroom.

Much to Shaw's displeasure, however, several other communities entered the contest. A contender by the name of Child's Landing won the hand. Benjamin Child, the town's founder, had sweetened his offer by including five acres of land and fifty thousand bricks. The real reason for his town being selected by the voters perhaps was that he hosted a free "come on down" barbecue and invited all residents of the county for a pre-election tour of Child's Landing.

Shaw and his cronies fumed and fussed about Child's blatant pandering to the voters, but to no avail. The citizens of Calhoun County poked a barbecue sauce-covered thumb in Boss Shaw's eye and voted to make Child's Landing (later renamed Hardin) the county seat.

An Illustrated History | 23

The courthouse is actually three buildings. The original building (far left) was built in 1858. A record storage building was added in 1895 (far right). The middle section, with columns, connects the two buildings. The middle building was added during the 1940s. A second story was built during the 1950s. Mount Carroll's only public hanging happened on the courthouse lawn. Joseph O'Neil, the condemned man, nearly escaped using his hands and a tin cup, but his tunnel was discovered only moments before he could dig himself free. He was executed on May 16, 1873.

Carroll County

Organized: February 22, 1839

County Seat: Mount Carroll

Named for: Charles Carroll, Founding Father

In 1839, Savanna had the largest population of any town in Carroll County. It was not favored to become the county seat because it was not located near the center of the county, but because of the number of voters who lived there, the town won the election with a slim forty-one vote majority. Victory was short-lived, however. Calls for a new election to select a town closer to the center of the county soon arose. In 1843, Mount Carroll became the new county seat.

The county's first courthouse at Mount Carroll was erected in 1843 on land donated by David Emmert, the owner of a flour grist mill. The structure was a modest, two-story, stone building with a small cupola. The building also served as the town's gathering place for social and religious meetings.

By the mid-1850s, the small building could no longer accommodate the needs of the expanding community. It was replaced in 1858 with a Classical-Revival structure that was designed by Chicago architects William Olmstead and Peter Nicholson. The Hallett Brick Yard, a local supplier, provided the bricks that were used to build the building.

In 1895, a separate "fireproof" building was built adjacent to the courthouse to house the county's records. In 1942, the two buildings were joined by the construction of a central structure.

A sketch of the 1858 courthouse illustrates a bicentennial year calendar. The courthouse was renovated and expanded in 1975 under supervision of the architectural firm of Johnson, Kile, Seehausen and Associates. (Artist: David Philmlee)

24 | Illinois Courthouses

Top Left: The 1845 courthouse at Beardstown was the site of the famous "Duff Armstrong Trial." Abraham Lincoln succeeded in clearing his client of a murder charge by use of an Old Farmer's Almanac. (Photo: Library of Congress—Historic American Buildings Survey, 1937)

Top Right: The 1875 building is the second courthouse in Virginia. The first courthouse there was occupied only briefly before the county seat was relocated at Beardstown. East and west wings were added to the core building in 1891.

Cass County

Organized: March 3, 1837

County Seat: Virginia

Named for: Lewis Cass, U.S. Secretary of War and State

Cass County's first county seat was located at Beardstown. While the county was being established, however, the owners of the town apparently decided to ignore one of the vital instructions issued by the General Assembly when they authorized its creation. There was a clause in the bill that ordered the city to pay the county $10,000 (to be paid in cash, land of equal value, or some combination of the two) in exchange for being named as the county seat. That payment was to be used for building a courthouse. The city fathers decided to rent space for the county court instead.

This misinterpretation of the legislators' intentions did not go unnoticed by the good folks of Virginia, a more centrally-located town. In 1839, they seized upon the issue and used it as leverage with the General Assembly. Their argument prevailed and Virginia was named as the new county seat. Henry Hall donated fifteen acres and lots were sold to finance the construction of a courthouse. On September 2, 1839, the Virginia courthouse was ready for occupancy.

Meanwhile, the Beardstown chieftains applied political leverage of their own with the General Assembly. Within several terms, they got the legislators to rescind their Virginia ruling and put the question to a public vote. Beardstown won that election and in 1845 the county seat was returned to their town. However, their hold on the county seat honor from then on was tenuous at best. In the next few years they made only tentative moves to expand or improve the town's hurriedly constructed courthouse. There was only trepid support for keeping the county seat at Beardstown.

Finally, in 1872, the state legislators once again ordered the county seat question to be placed before the voters. Virginia won that election.

The second Virginia courthouse was occupied in the summer of 1875. The county seat has remained there ever since and the building has been expanded several times.

An Illustrated History | 25

Champaign County

Organized: February 20, 1833

County Seat: Urbana

Named for: Champaign County, Ohio

Architect Joseph Royer designed the 1899 building with a budget of $150,000 (about $3,370,000 in 2007).

The first courthouse in Champaign County was constructed in Urbana soon after Governor John Reynolds's signature was dry on the formal organization papers. The hewn-log building was considered crude even by the rough and ready standards of the frontier. Court was held in the structure during the 1836–1837 terms, but, in 1840, the building was razed and replaced by a more adequate brick and wood frame structure.

The third courthouse, built in 1849, was a two-story, frame construction with a bell tower. That building was remodeled in 1860 at a cost of $30,000 (about $600,000 in 2007). The exterior was covered with brick and iron beams were added to strengthen the frame of the building.

26 | Illinois Courthouses

The courthouse tower featured a tall spire that was shortened and finally removed between 1930 and 1952. A Seth Thomas 1877 clockwork was installed in the third courthouse on November 10, 1883. The National Standard Time system began at noon on November 18, 1883. There is an effort afoot to restore the clock tower to its original height.

COURT-HOUSE, CHAMPAIGN CO., URBANA

Perhaps even more important than the remodeling of the building was the decision to construct a horse-drawn "interurban" rail trolley system to connect the county seat with a new railroad depot—named Champaign—that had been built along the tracks that ran two miles west of Urbana. The interurban line connected the two towns and short-circuited a call to shift the county seat to Champaign.

In 1899, the county officials announced plans to build a new courthouse. Architect Joseph Royer was hired to design the building. His stately structure was constructed of sandstone and mottled brick. It featured a tower that stood 135 feet high. The building was dedicated in 1901. The tower was struck many times by lightning, resulting in the loss of its spire in 1930 and removal of the entire upper section of the tower in 1952. Royer, who was still a practicing architect, designed a parapet to replace the tower's spire.

That building continues to serve the county, but in 2002 the building was greatly expanded with a new addition. The firms of Isaksen & Glerum Architects, and Moyer Associates designed the addition and remodeling project.

Christian County

Organized: February 15, 1839

County Seat: Taylorville

Named for: Christian County, Kentucky

Left: The square tower on the 1901 courthouse is 140 feet tall.

Above: Gregory M. Hosto, senior deputy, guides visitors to the top of the courthouse tower. The Howard Company clock still keeps perfect time.

Christian County's original name was Dane County in honor of Nathan Dane, a member of the U.S. Congress who guided the passage of a 1787 ordinance that prohibited the expansion of slavery into the Northwest Territory. Dane fell into disfavor after the 1804 Louisiana Purchase, which doubled the size of the United States overnight. Southern legislators then began to argue that any new states formed in the future might want to decide for themselves whether or not to allow slavery. By 1840, the Missouri Compromise of 1820 was tattered and teetering. The county officials decided to drop Dane and adopt Christian.

The first courthouse was authorized in 1839 and completed in 1840. A court order was necessary to force the owners of the town to make good on their $1,000 pledge to help construct a courthouse. The corporation settled its debt by deeding seventy-eight lots to the county. Abraham Lincoln practiced law in the 1839 courthouse and a replica building has been preserved as a Lincoln memorial at New Salem.

The second courthouse was ready for occupancy in 1856. Contractors Dennis and Ream built it at a cost of $13,526 (about $260,000 in 2007).

In 1900, the county supervisors asked the voters to pass a levy to build the present courthouse. The levy was approved and, in 1901, the building committee chose a design by J. W. Gaddis, a well-known and respected courthouse architect from Terre Haute. The courthouse is 117 feet long, 90 feet wide, and three stories high. Cost of the building, including furniture, came to $100,535.80 (about $2,130,000 in 2007).

Left: The 1839 courthouse served until 1856. Abe Lincoln supposedly helped chase pigs from under this courthouse. The grunts from the noisy swine made it impossible for the judge to hear the lawyers in the courtroom. (Artist: Robert Johnson)

Right: The county's second courthouse (1856–1901). (Artist: Robert Johnson)

An Illustrated History | 29

Clark County

Organized: March 22, 1819

County Seat: Marshall

Named for: George Rogers Clark, Governor of the Northwest Territory

The architectural firm of Fuller and Hawkes designed the 1904 courthouse.

In 1819, Clark County's first county seat was located at Aurora Bend on the Wabash River—a town that since has faded out of existence. The county's business and court sessions were transacted in the parlor of a log cabin that was borrowed or rented for the purpose.

In 1823, the county seat was transferred to Darwin, another town situated on the Wabash. The county built a hewn-log courthouse there in 1827, but that town's location also failed to meet the people's expectations. In 1837, the state legislators appointed three commissioners to search for another site that was more centrally located in the county. The seat of justice was moved to Marshall.

The first Marshall courthouse was erected in 1839. It was a sturdy frame building. In 1887, it was razed to make way for a new courthouse. That courthouse, unfortunately, suffered a devastating fire in 1902. It was built with brick, supposedly a "fireproof" material, but a discarded match or smoldering cigar butt touched off a blaze that gutted the building.

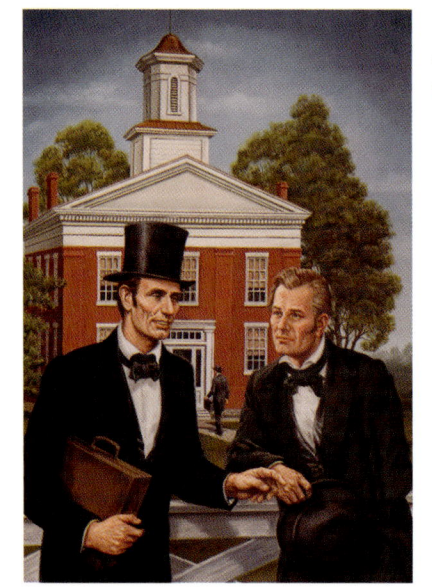

The county's fifth and present courthouse was built at a cost of $60,000 (about $1,150,000 in 2007). The building was occupied on July 2, 1904.

The 1839 courthouse was notable as the site of an 1850 trial in which Lincoln helped defend William D. Davis against a murder charge. It was considered a successful defense because the charge was reduced to manslaughter and Davis was sentenced to only three years in prison. (Artist: Lloyd Ostendorf)

30 | Illinois Courthouses

Clay County

Organized: December 23, 1824

County Seat: Louisville

Named for: Henry Clay, Kentucky Senator

Architect J. W. Royer designed the 1912 courthouse.

Political machinations were stirring in 1825 when Clay County's first county seat was established. The men who selected the site decided to name it "Hubbardsville," presumably in honor of Governor A. F. Hubbard. The organizational meeting minutes of March 1825 show Hubbardsville as the town's name.

Hubbard, who actually was the lieutenant governor, was filling in for Edward Coles, Illinois' second governor, for several weeks while Coles was out of the state on business. Hubbard, a politician whose grasp fell short of his reach, tried to usurp the governor's office by claiming that Coles had vacated the office by leaving the state. The Illinois Supreme Court quickly straightened out the question of gubernatorial succession and Hubbard's political star twinkled into oblivion, never to shine again.

When the Clay County Commissioners met a few months later in June of 1825, they quietly erased the name Hubbardsville and wrote in Maysville as the name of the county seat. Daniel May earlier had donated twenty acres for the county seat site and built the first courthouse.

In 1841, the county seat was relocated to Louisville. Court sessions were held in a rented room during the 1842 term. Construction on the first courthouse was started in 1843 but, when contractor Samuel Slocumb presented his bill for $35.99 (about $857 in 2007), the county refused to take possession of the structure. The building remained unfinished until 1846. The county hired Hartwig Samuelson to complete the job.

In 1861, the citizens of Flora called for an election in hopes of having the county seat transferred to their city, a booming railroad town situated near the southern border of the county. The legislature authorized an election to decide the issue but Flora's inconvenient location doomed its hopes at the polls.

In 1912, the Flora natives tried a second time to seize the county seat honor when the county officials announced repairs needed to be made to the courthouse. It was a poorly kept secret that the officials planned to use their "remodeling project" as a sneaky way to build a new courthouse without asking the voters to approve the expense. News of the courthouse gang's hanky-panky stirred up discontent and the Flora folks were optimistic that voters would punish the courthouse hooligans by moving the county seat to their town.

Alas, despite their whistle-blowing, Flora again was passed over by the electorate and the old courthouse was razed to make way for a new building that was erected in its place.

Clinton County

Organized: December 27, 1824

County Seat: Carlyle

Named for: DeWitt Clinton, Governor of New York

Above: The 1999 Clinton County Courthouse was designed by the architectural firms of Kuhlmann Design Group and Phillips Swager Associates.

Below: Clinton County's second courthouse served from 1849 to 1997.

In 1819, before Clinton County was separated from Washington County, its major town of Carlyle was a candidate to be named as Illinois' state capital. The state constitution of 1818 specified that the legislators petition the U.S. Congress for land somewhere upstream on the Kaskaskia River. The Illinois territory capital was at Kaskaskia, a town on the banks of the Mississippi River. It became the state capital by default when statehood was granted in 1818 but there was never an intention that it would remain as the capital for very long.

Carlyle and another town called Pope's Bluff were the two towns being given serious consideration by the General Assembly. But, before a choice could be made, a man began telling the state legislators about another site, a village that was a little farther up the Kaskaskia called Reeve's Bluff. His sales pitch must have been one for the record books because, in 1820, Reeve's Bluff was named as Illinois' second state capital. The town was renamed Vandalia.

When Clinton County was organized in 1824, it was well on its way to becoming settled—some 33,000 acres already had been claimed, three-fifths by actual settlers and the balance by land speculators. Carlyle, even though it had been passed over as the new state capital, was named as the county seat and has remained so from that day.

32 | Illinois Courthouses

Coles County

Organized: December 25, 1830

County Seat: Charleston

Named for: Edward Coles, Illinois' Second Governor

Above: The 1898 courthouse was designed by architect C. W. Rapp.

Below Top: The 1835 courthouse was a "foursquare" building, a common design of the times and so-called because of the equal length of the walls.

Below Bottom: The 1835 courthouse's basic design was remodeled by adding wings and a portico during the Civil War era.

In 1830, Coles County was triple its present geographic size. Two new counties were created later from its bulk: Cumberland County to the south and Douglas County to the north. Despite those changes in the size of the county's footprint, the town of Charleston has remained the county seat throughout.

The first courthouse was built in 1831. It was made with hewn logs and furnished with hand-carved wooden benches. The second courthouse, built in 1835, was constructed with brick and built in the foursquare architectural style favored by many courthouse officials of the age. Shortly before the outbreak of the Civil War, about 1858, the courthouse was enlarged by adding a wing and installing a portico supported by four brick pillars. A second wing was added to the building in 1864, restoring balance to the structure.

Protest surrounded the construction of the 1898 courthouse. The commissioners had told people they only intended to "repair" the old 1835 courthouse. As soon as the project had begun, however, the old building was razed to make way for an entirely new courthouse. Some voters of the county were irate when they were then asked to pay for a new building they had not approved in advance. The cost of constructing the new building probably was about the same as remodeling the old one, but the lack of transparency rankled the citizenry's sense of fair play. And, the maneuver short-changed the other communities in the county who might have wanted to vie for the county seat honor, a common occurrence whenever voters were asked to underwrite the cost of building a new courthouse. But, that may have been the reason for the clandestine approach in the first place.

Despite the criticism reported in the press at the time, the 1898 courthouse was a handsome, well-built building that continues to serve the county into the twenty-first century.

An Illustrated History

Cook County

Organized: January 15, 1831

County Seat: Chicago

Named for: Daniel P. Cook, Illinois' First Attorney General

Top Left: The Daley Center was built in 1965. Architect C. F. Murphy Associates designed the building. The skyscraper courthouse is just one of the many buildings, facilities, and annexes that house the county's vast network of judicial, law enforcement, and administrative services.

Top Right: Spanish artist Pablo Picasso (1881–1973) donated the enigmatic sculpture that was added to the plaza in 1967. One of the most famous and recognized pieces of public art in America, the statue is made of Cor-Ten, the same self-weathering steel that was used to construct the Daley Center.

When Cook County was organized in 1831 most of the people who came to Illinois were homesteading in the southern one-third of the state. Buffalo herds and Native American tribes still passed back and forth across the northern two-thirds of Illinois. There were fewer than one hundred white residents in the 946 square mile county. The county seat was at Fort Dearborn, a small army outpost that had been built in 1803.

The U.S. Army had evacuated the fort during the War of 1812 and it was burned by Indians. Rebuilt in 1816, the sleepy outpost experienced little action during the next twenty years as the soldiers enjoyed peaceful relations with the Native American tribes in the region. Beyond the fort's wooden palisade, fur trappers and traders paddled their canoes down the Chicago River, searching for beaver and wild game.

Civilization arrived in 1831. That was the year when three commissioners of the newly organized Cook County Board met for two days at Fort Dearborn to set up the basic structure of a county government. The men elected a sheriff and a few other county officers. Their last duty that day before retiring to the fort's grog house for refreshment was to draft a letter requesting the state to give the county about ten acres of public land. They planned to sell lots from that acreage to generate enough cash to erect a jail and courthouse. The commissioners were cautiously optimistic about the future of Cook County thanks primarily to the success of the Erie Canal.

Right: A combined courthouse and city hall building was erected in 1853 and stood at the corner of LaSalle and Randolph streets. Lincoln's body lay in state in this building after his assassination. The building was destroyed by the 1871 fire. (Library of Congress American Memory Section - Chicago Daily News collection)

Bottom Left: The 1906 city hall and courthouse were located at 121 North LaSalle Street and was designed by the architectural firm of Holabird and Roche. Many sensational trials were conducted in this building, including the infamous 1924 trial of the Leopold and Loeb murder of Bobby Franks. It is no longer used as a government building.

Bottom Right: In 1831, a small settlement in the shadow of Fort Dearborn served as the county seat. Chicago was incorporated in 1833 and chartered by the state in 1837. The name of the city is based on an Algonquian word that means "place of the onion," from the wild onions growing there.

The Erie Canal opened to traffic in 1825 and the freight and passenger business already was paying big dividends for the modest New York state cities of Buffalo and New York City. The canal connected the New York harbor with Lake Erie, the entry point to the Great Lakes. By 1831, Illinois' more progressive legislators were sketching out plans for constructing a similar canal in Illinois—one that would carry goods and people from Lake Michigan to the Mississippi River—and then on to New Orleans.

Fort Dearborn's sleepy days were coming to an end and the birth of a new city—Chicago—was about to transform a remote outpost into a commercial powerhouse.

Based on the most recent census numbers, Cook County now contains more than eight hundred local governmental units. The city's population is approaching three million and it is the third largest city in the United States. The metropolitan area has approximately ten million people, making Cook County the second most populous county in the nation and the nineteenth largest government in the United States.

An Illustrated History | 35

The Great Chicago Fire

Chicago in 1871 was the midwestern hub for Great Lakes shipping and railroad traffic. The Great Fire destroyed the central business district and many neighborhoods around the core of the city. (Artwork: Library of Congress, Geography and Map Division)

Once upon a time, a wind-driven conflagration came perilously close to erasing Chicago from the map of Cook County. The blaze started about nine o'clock on Sunday, October 8, 1871. Flames were first seen in a barn behind the home of Patrick and Catherine O'Leary at 13 De Koven Street. Folklore credits a cow with kicking over a lantern, but no one knows for sure how the hell-storm began.

The city's firefighting crews, already exhausted from fighting a large fire the day before, were first sent to the wrong neighborhood. When they finally arrived at the O'Leary's house, the fire already was out of control.

Dry winds fanned the flames east and north through the city. The community's humblest homes, most ornate mansions, government buildings, schoolhouses, famous mercantile establishments, and factories of all types were destined to become tinder for the all consuming blaze. The fire raged out of control for two days. There was no relief until a thunderstorm finally quenched the flames. At least three hundred people were killed, one hundred thousand people were left homeless, and property worth $200 million (more than $3 billion in 2007) was reduced to ashes. Many of the federal records and county legal documents that had been stored at the Cook County Courthouse for safekeeping were lost.

The 1871 Chicago fire was one of the most spectacular events of the nineteenth century, and it still ranks as one of the nation's worst natural disasters.

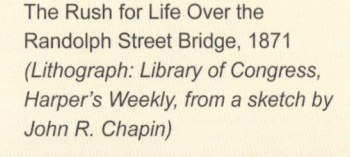

The Rush for Life Over the Randolph Street Bridge, 1871 (Lithograph: Library of Congress, Harper's Weekly, from a sketch by John R. Chapin)

36 | Illinois Courthouses

Crawford County

Organized: December 31, 1816

County Seat: Robinson

Named for: William H. Crawford, U.S. Secretary of War

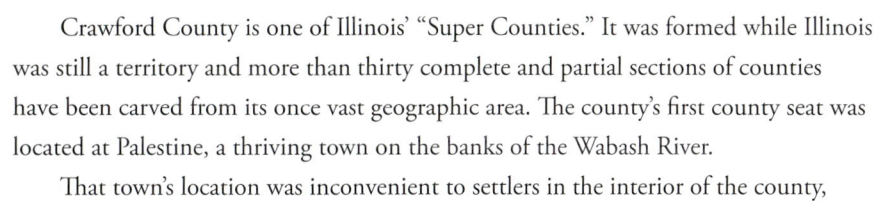

Crawford County is one of Illinois' "Super Counties." It was formed while Illinois was still a territory and more than thirty complete and partial sections of counties have been carved from its once vast geographic area. The county's first county seat was located at Palestine, a thriving town on the banks of the Wabash River.

That town's location was inconvenient to settlers in the interior of the county, however, and citizens petitioned to move the county seat to a more central location. The General Assembly approved the request and, on Christmas Day 1843, ground was cleared at the town of Robinson for the purpose of building a public square and courthouse. William Baker donated eighty acres of land for the project.

The first courthouse was a temporary structure, a small frame building. The jail that had been built of hewn logs at Palestine was dismantled and moved to Robinson. In 1844, a permanent brick courthouse was completed at a cost of $4,200 (about $97,300 in 2007). The courthouse was a two-story building with a decorative cupola atop its hipped roof.

The 1895 courthouse's cornerstone was dedicated on October 24 and completed in 1896. Architect J. W. Gaddis designed the building. Unfortunately, the central bell tower, peaked caps that topped the corner towers of the building, and the conical caps on the twin turrets at the entrance were removed during the twentieth century due to a fire in 1899.

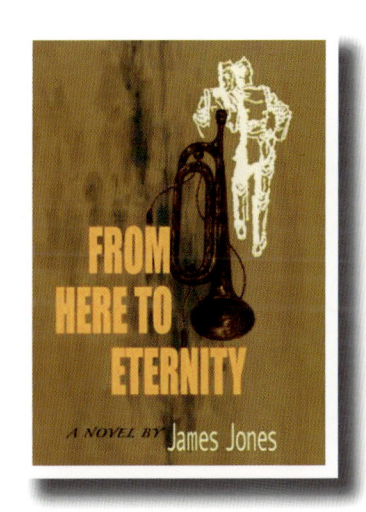

Top: An engineering survey conducted in 2000 determined that the building's walls are structurally sound and capable of withstanding the stress of replacing the original roof line and tower. A private fundraising effort is underway to rebuild the building's tower.

Inset Above: The 1895 courthouse suffered a fire on March 28, 1899. The core building was saved but the pitched roof had to be removed and the tower was dismantled.

James Jones (1921–1977), a native son of Crawford County, authored several acclaimed World War II related novels. At the end of the war, he returned to Robinson and stayed with friends while writing his classic novel, From Here to Eternity.

An Illustrated History | 37

Cumberland County

Organized: March 2, 1843

County Seat: Toledo

Named for: The Cumberland (National) Road

Top: A bandstand with a jaunty cupola brightens the lawn of the 1887 courthouse.

Inset Right: The 1855 courthouse.

While it still was part of Coles County, Cumberland County was a swampy area interspersed with patches of prairie grass that stood taller than an elephant's eye. The first wave of settlers snapped up the land at bargain prices and energetically drained the boggy land, transforming it into reasonably tillable farmland. The county was organized as a separate political entity in 1843.

State legislators picked the town of Greenup to act as the temporary county seat until an election could be held. DeKalb won that contest but Greenup continued to serve as the county seat. Some vested persons claimed that the titles for land that were to be used by the county at DeKalb were murky.

In 1855, the county's residents held a second election and Toledo was chosen as the new county seat. Toledo had wanted the honor from the start and, some suspect, may have been involved in questioning whether or not land titles at DeKalb were clear of encumbrances. Such was the hardball that was played in the quest for county seat honors.

No Greenup courthouse had ever been built so the county's first courthouse was erected in Toledo in 1855. Wiley Ross and Bennet Beals were the builders, but their work moved forward relatively slowly because a pond on the construction site had to be drained first.

The foursquare, two-story building had three doors, nineteen windows, and a cupola with a bell that could be heard for five miles. That building burned in 1885. The current courthouse, completed in 1887, continues to serve the county.

DeKalb County

Organized: March 4, 1837

County Seat: Sycamore

Named for: Johann DeKalb, Revolutionary War General

Top: The architectural firm of Watson & Hazleton provided the plans for the 1903 DeKalb County Courthouse which feature an impressive pediment at the front of the building. In 1986, the building was restored under the supervision of the architectural firm of Burnside, Cassell & Associates.

Inset Above: The main courtroom, with its impressive skylight, is maintained in like new condition after more than one hundred years of use.

Politicians and land speculators schemed lustily and maneuvered mightily in their efforts to have their own favorite town named as the county seat. While the deals were being discussed, court was held at a temporary seat of justice established in the town of Coltonville. Rufus Colton, the town's founder, happened also to be the county clerk and perhaps influenced the selection of his town for the honor, but his efforts were to no avail in the long run. Through a series of run-off elections the various contenders were eliminated until eventually the town of Sycamore triumphed. The victory was a solid one and the town has been DeKalb County's only county seat.

In 1839, the county built a courthouse in Sycamore. It was a 20 by 30 foot, two-story, roughly appointed building. County Clerk Colton, perhaps still feeling prickly because his town had been passed over as the county seat, insisted that the building was unfit to be used and argued that court should continue to be held at his home in Coltonville. Soon the patience of the other county officials grew thin and they sought a circuit court judge's opinion in the matter. The judge ruled that the Sycamore building would have to serve, even in its less than pristine condition.

In 1850, a second courthouse was built. That was a 40 by 60 foot, two-story, brick building with a cupola clock tower. Money in the county treasury was tight and the budget was set at $6,000 (about $124,000 in 2007). The county scraped together funds by selling the old courthouse, a common practice at that time, and by auctioning its remaining real estate property in Sycamore. The county was still short of the required amount, however, and private donors pledged the final 25 percent needed to finish the project. William Phelps was the contractor. An annex was added in 1863.

In the late 1890s, when word of building a new courthouse was announced, a contest erupted between DeKalb and Sycamore over which town should be the county seat. An election was held to decide the question but the results were tainted by excessive ballot box stuffing in both communities.

Legal protests and injunctions swirled back and forth, but Sycamore's citizens took a leap of faith and in October 1903 authorized the construction of a new courthouse. As construction was underway, the legal contest dragged on through the lower courts until, in 1905, it reached the Illinois Supreme Court. The justices ruled in favor of Sycamore just as the newly completed courthouse was dedicated with appropriate hoopla and sighs of relief.

An Illustrated History | 39

DeWitt County

Organized: March 1, 1839

County Seat: Clinton

Named for: DeWitt Clinton, a Governor of New York

Above Left: The present courthouse was dedicated in 1986. It was designed by the firm of FGM, Incorporated.

Above: Clinton's second courthouse was a basic two-story, brick building constructed around 1849. Circuit rider Lincoln and Clifton Moore practiced law in that courthouse. In 1860, Moore played a major role in securing the Republican Party's candidacy for Lincoln. (Artist: Lloyd Ostendorf)

Below: The county's third courthouse was built around the turn of the century and bore a remarkable resemblance to the Pike County Courthouse.

The General Assembly's act that authorized the formation of DeWitt County specified that the town selected as the county seat had to pay $2,000 for construction of public buildings within the first two years of the county seat being located in that community. Once anointed, the town could satisfy its obligation either by paying cash or by donating land of equal market value. Donating land was the option most often used, leaving it up to the county to auction the land to raise cash for constructing public buildings.

The towns of Clinton and DeWitt vied with each other to be selected as the county seat. Neither town would back down so a run-off election had to be held to pick a winner. Clinton, the more centrally-located town, won.

Abe Lincoln's 1860 election to the White House may have begun in Clinton thanks to his friendship with Clifton H. Moore that evolved while the two men practiced law at the county courthouse. Moore was the first lawyer to settle in Clinton and by the age of thirty-four had become a wealthy man through his law practice and by engaging in land speculation deals. Lincoln visited the town twice each year for more than twenty years as a lawyer riding the old Eighth Judicial Circuit and the two men became good friends.

Moore had become a pillar in the Republican Party, the new political group that arose in 1854 from the ashes of the defunct Whig Party. The party held its national convention in Chicago in 1860 and Moore was one of the key men maneuvering on Lincoln's behalf at the gathering of party delegates. The race for the nomination to be the party's presidential candidate was packed with nationally known front runners, but none could muster the necessary votes to go over the top. Moore masterminded the compromise that allowed Lincoln, a "dark horse" candidate, to break the deadlock and secure the nomination. After Lincoln was elected president, Moore undoubtedly could have had any high government position for the asking, but he declined any reward, save his friendship with Lincoln.

Douglas County

Organized: February 8, 1859

County Seat: Tuscola

Named for: Stephen A. Douglas

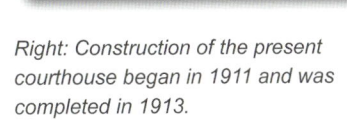

Right: Construction of the present courthouse began in 1911 and was completed in 1913.

Inset Above: The 1864 courthouse was designed by architect O. L. Kinney.

Above Top: A terra cotta mold of Stephen Douglas's face is displayed in the courthouse lobby. Douglas was a national leader of the Democratic Party and one of Illinois' most popular politicians. The county was named in his honor while he was still alive, a rare occurrence. (Bust modeled by Bell & Hermant of Chicago)

In 1861, the county erected its first courthouse, a modest, two-story, frame structure. The cost of construction was provided by private donations and amounted to $1,900 (about $36,600 in 2007).

In 1864, construction began on the county's second courthouse. That building had more ambitious architectural aspirations. It was three-stories tall, with an octagonal tower that was topped with a cupola. An observation catwalk encircled the tower, giving the tower structure an appearance that was somewhat akin to a lighthouse.

This courthouse cost $42,000 (about $498,000 in 2007). Overall, it was an attractive structure but unfortunately developed expensive repair defects. The jail situated in the basement of the building soon was considered unsafe and other maintenance issues kept cropping up. Taxpayers became annoyed at the building because they were assessed on an almost annual basis to pay for repairs.

The 1911 courthouse cost $170,000 (about $2.9 million in 2007). It was designed by architect Joseph Royer. His fee was $7,550 (about $170,000 in 2007).

An Illustrated History | 41

DuPage County

Organized: February 9, 1839

County Seat: Wheaton

Named for: The DuPage River

The 1990 DuPage County Courthouse is part of a sprawling, park-like complex. These government offices serve the second largest court system in Illinois.

DuPage County was organized in the early months of 1839 and Naperville was selected as the county seat. A courthouse was promptly built there. In 1848, after a railroad line was built at the rival town of Wheaton, the two communities entered into a bitter and protracted skirmish over which should be the county seat.

In 1857, the issue was placed before the voters to decide and Naperville won that round of the fight. A decade later, with tempers still high, the question again was placed before the voters. That 1867 election turned violent. Mobs roamed the streets, looking for trouble, and one man was killed in a scuffle after being hit in the head with a rock.

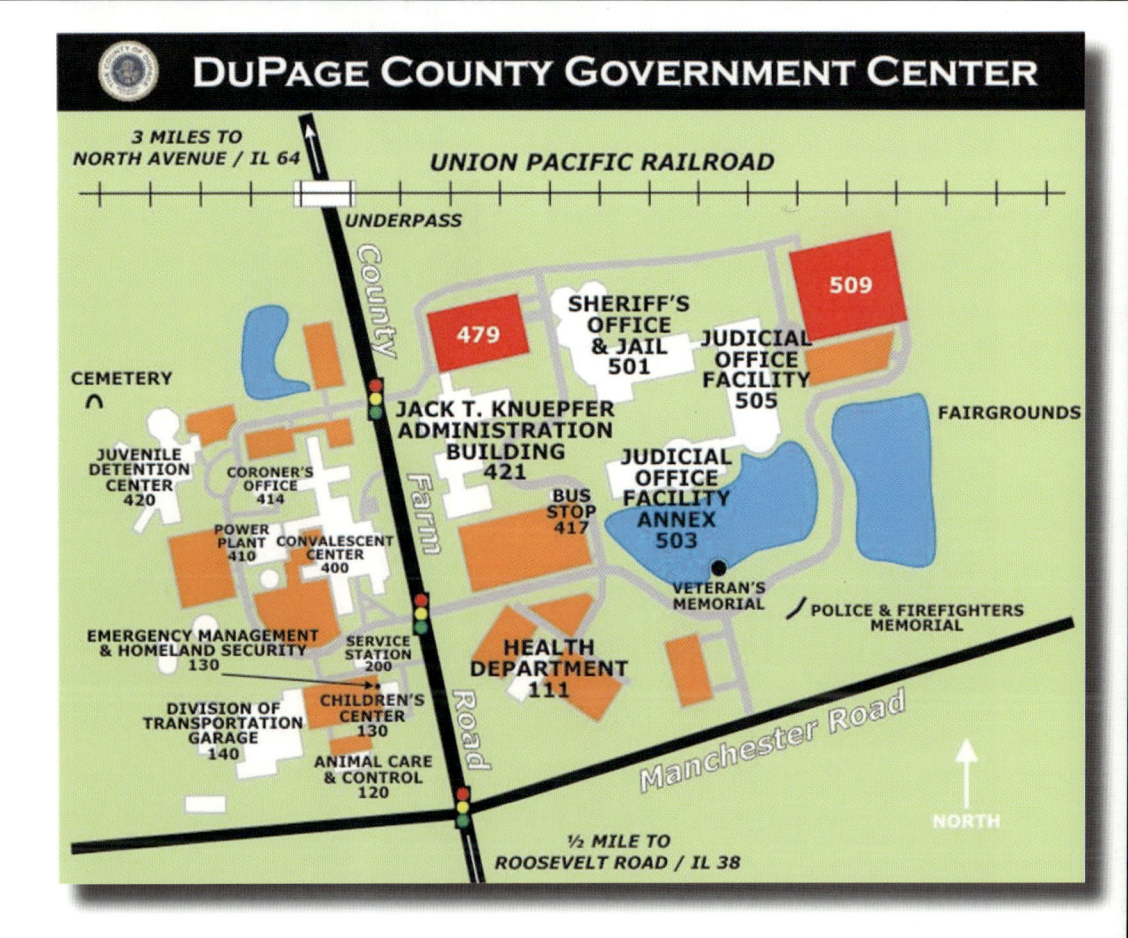

Below Top: Wheaton built its first courthouse in 1867 while still locked in a heated contest with Naperville over the question of which town was the authentic county seat.

Below Bottom: The second Wheaton courthouse was erected in 1896 and was remodeled in 1952.

Despite the violence, Wheaton claimed victory by a margin of twenty-nine votes. They immediately began construction of a courthouse. Meanwhile, Naperville's infuriated citizens claimed there had been fraud at the ballot box. County business came to a standstill for several months while the towns filed for court injunctions against one another. At one point during the stand-off, a group of hotheads from Wheaton broke into the Naperville courthouse and carried off all but six volumes of the county records. Naperville vigilantes caught the raiding party as they were making their getaway and recovered most of the records. The amateur burglars dropped the record books in their haste to outrun their bloodthirsty pursuers.

After the break-in was thwarted, the Naperville officials decided to move the county records to Chicago for safekeeping at the Cook County clerk's office. Tragically, this plan miscarried—the Chicago Fire of 1871 destroyed all of the county's records.

Eventually the General Assembly mediated the feud and ruled in favor of Wheaton's claim. In 1896, a second Wheaton courthouse was built and that building served until 1990 when the present courthouse located within the sprawling government complex was dedicated.

An Illustrated History | 43

The 1891 courthouse is clad with Amherst stone, a beige or off-white-colored sandstone. There are four entrances to the building.

Edgar County

Organized: January 3, 1823

County Seat: Paris

Named for: John Edgar, an early Illinois pioneer

The town of Paris was selected as the county seat because of its location near the geographic center of Edgar County. Samuel Vance sealed the deal by donating twenty-six acres to the county. In 1825, the county constructed a modest courthouse. It was a 22 by 32 foot, two-story, weatherboard covered building that was topped with a cupola.

In 1833, the county commissioners authorized construction of a second courthouse. It was a more substantial brick building. It was built by Leander Munsell for $4,250 (about $104,000 in 2007).

A painting of the Palace of Mechanical Arts hangs on the second floor above the main staircase. The Palace was one of the exhibit halls of the 1893 World's Columbian Exposition, more commonly referred to as the Chicago Worlds Fair. The architecture at the fair sparked interest in a return to the classical styles that had been in vogue during the early years of the nineteenth century, and marked the decline of the heavier, more ornate courthouse styles that dominated the latter half of that century. (Artist unknown)

The courtroom in this courthouse was available to be used for social and religious meetings whenever court was not in session. The courthouse almost always was the largest building in a frontier community and quickly became the city's gathering place and social center. Clubs, church congregations, and civil groups would eventually have the wherewithal to build their own meeting halls and churches but in the meantime it was common practice for those groups to use the courthouse for meetings.

Abraham Lincoln and Stephen Douglas both visited the Edgar County Courthouse, but never at the same time. Douglas spoke there in 1855 on the slavery issue. He did not argue in favor of slavery, per se, but rather that local citizens should be allowed to decide such issues rather than have the decision made for them by the federal government. Douglas's argument—"local sovereignty" was a plank in the Democratic Party's platform—was ethically bankrupt, but legalistically defensible during a time when half of the nation's economy depended upon the immoral practice of trafficking in human beings.

Lincoln practiced law and visited the courthouse frequently during his years as a circuit riding lawyer. In 1858, while campaigning against Douglas for a U.S. Senate seat, he spoke at a rally there.

The courthouse was razed in 1883 and court was held for several years in rented rooms and halls. In 1891, the citizens voted to build their third and current structure. The courthouse was designed by architect Henry Elliott and dedicated in 1893.

An Illustrated History | 45

Edwards County

Organized: November 28, 1814

County Seat: Albion

Named for: Ninian Edwards, Governor of the Illinois Territory

Above: The clock in the tower of the 1888 courthouse was a gift of appreciation from the town of Albion. The building was erected after the voters had rejected passage of a bond election and then surreptitiously agreed to a massive "remodeling" of the old courthouse. The 1859 jail building, far right, is maintained as a museum.

In 1814, the town of Palmyra was picked to be the county seat, but popular support was lukewarm. After a few years of complaints, the newly formed (1818) state legislature agreed to authorize elections to decide if the seat of justice should be moved from Palmyra to a more convenient site in the county.

The town fathers of Albion, one of the towns competing to be the people's choice for the county seat, agreed to donate the customary acreage to the county, but they sweetened the offer by promising to toss in seventy thousand bricks, and all of the stone, boards, nails, and other materials that would be needed to actually build a courthouse. This sounded pretty much like a free courthouse to the voters. Albion won the run-off election in a walk and became Edwards County's seat of justice in 1821.

Right: Local contractor Elias Weaver built the 1852 courthouse and the jail a few years later. The two buildings stood side by side and were harmonious in style. The courthouse was razed to make way for the 1888 courthouse.

In July 1823, the county contracted with John Robinson and William Wilkinson to build a one-story courthouse. A year later, August 1824, the commissioners amended the construction order by adding a second story to the building and increasing its size from 26 by 30 feet to 50 by 30 feet, effectively doubling the size of the building. They decided to add a cupola to the structure as well. It is not clear at what stage of construction the builders were in when the specifications were revised so drastically, but probably not so far as to necessitate dismantling an almost finished building and starting over. This courthouse was completed in May 1825.

In 1852 the county built its second courthouse. Elias Weaver was hired to build the structure and a few years later, in 1859, he built a new jail for the county as well.

Weaver's courthouse was condemned as unsafe in 1887. The commissioners decided to raze the dilapidated structure so they could build anew, and they placed a bond issue before the voters to pay for the work. The measure did not pass.

After the election, talk drifted back to citizens living at the county seat about the possibility of other communities seeking an election in hopes of moving the county seat to a new location. Such dangerous gossip caused the folks of Albion to pause and reflect and, before long, a party of community leaders approached the commissioners with a strange request. They asked the county officials to ignore the "no" vote on a new courthouse and instead order a "remodeling" of the existing courthouse. Wink, wink. The term remodeling in this instance was understood by one and all as a complicit go-ahead from the citizenry for the commissioners to raze the old building and build anew. Armed with political cover, the officials were only too happy to oblige. The building committee accepted a design drawn by the McDonald Brothers and work began on the present courthouse in 1888.

In 1940, the county secured a WPA grant to build an addition on the courthouse. In 1997, the Garrison & Jones architectural firm supervised accessibility improvements and construction of a two-story, 10,700 square foot addition.

Effingham County

Organized: February 15, 1831

County Seat: Effingham

Named for: Lord Edward Effingham

The route of the National Road (aka the Cumberland Road) ran through the land that would eventually become Effingham County. The road building crews paused in the area long enough to build a bridge over the Little Wabash River. The bridge work took awhile and the workers built some crude shacks for shelter, creating a makeshift village. When most of the workers moved down the right of way to continue building the road, a few of the workers decided to stay in the cabins they had erected. Their rough camp on the Little Wabash become a town named Ewington.

Ewington prospered and it was selected as the county seat when Effingham County was organized. A hewn-log courthouse was built there in 1835 and that structure was replaced in 1844 by a foursquare brick building.

In the early 1850s the railroads thundered into Illinois and land speculation exploded. Investors bought thousands of acres of undeveloped land, trying to stay one hop ahead of the railroad lines that were crisscrossing the prairie. Every town wanted to be the site of the next depot on a railroad line.

Effingham, perhaps because of its proximity to the Cumberland Road, was dead center in the crosshairs of the junction of two rail lines, the Mississippi and Atlantic Railroad and the Illinois Central. Effingham prospered dramatically, and in 1860 the boom town easily won the county seat honor from nearby Ewington. A courthouse was quickly built in Effingham but that structure was destroyed by fire in 1869. Ewington soon was absorbed into Effingham's environs.

After the fire and loss of the courthouse, the usual agitation arose to move the county seat to a more central location. A public ruckus between city and county officials over who should pay the biggest share of the cost for a new courthouse added fuel to the squabble and made Effingham even more vulnerable to being displaced. Private donors quieted the waters by pledging money to build a new courthouse. That face-saving gesture by the local business community allowed both the city and county officials to claim victory for their constituents and doused the calls for relocating the county seat to a new venue.

The building committee chose plans submitted by William Brown and the courthouse's cornerstone was placed on July 15, 1870. That handsome building served until it was replaced by the current courthouse, which was dedicated in 2007. Paul Greco, an architect with the Durrant Company, drew the plans for the new courthouse. It was built at a site several blocks from the old town square, thereby allowing the old courthouse to be available for other purposes.

Top: The 2007 courthouse is closer to the city's downtown business district. The 1870 courthouse remains on the town square.

Above: The rounded cap that once crowned the tower has been removed from the old courthouse but otherwise architect Brown's 1870 design is intact.

Fayette County

Organized: February 14, 1821

County Seat: Vandalia

Named for: Marquis de la Fayette

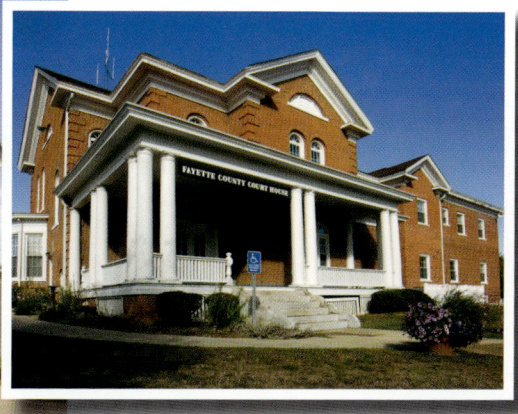

Top: The courthouse has been expanded several times. In 1995, several free standing buildings were connected and this new rounded entrance was added to the renovated structure.

Top Right: The courthouse was a private residence in 1932. The original front porch remains in place.

Above: The county used the old statehouse as its courthouse from 1840 until 1933. That building is now a state historical site.

When the General Assembly decided to move the state capital from Kaskaskia, they almost picked the town of Carlyle, in Clinton County, but instead selected Reeve's Bluff (later renamed Vandalia) a village a few miles further north on the Kaskaskia River. In doing so, the legislators waved the requirement that twenty acres needed to be donated to the county in exchange for Vandalia being named the county seat. That lifted one burden from Fayette County but on the other hand gave them no public land that could be auctioned to build a courthouse. Small price to pay, they thought, in exchange for being named as the state capital. County court sessions were held at a series of buildings in Vandalia, including a schoolroom, the county clerk's office, and some rented rooms. They never did get around to building a courthouse.

Vandalia was the Illinois capital from 1819 to 1839. The first two statehouses were modest and plainly built structures. In the mid-1830s pressure arose to move the state government to a more center of the state location. In 1834, a petition was circulated that criticized the city's unsuitability as a state capital and suggested that Illinois would be better off if the capital were to be relocated at Springfield. Unnerved by this request, Vandalia's civic leaders decided to build a new, more refined statehouse, trying to improve the city's image with the lawmakers. The city's third statehouse was unveiled in 1836. But, it was too late to make a good first impression. Legislators, including Abraham Lincoln and the other members of "Long Nine" caucus, persisted until Springfield was named as the new state capital in December 1839.

The legislators surrendered the empty statehouse to Fayette County for use as a courthouse. It served in that capacity until the early 1930s when the state bought it to restore it as a state historic memorial. The county began searching for a new courthouse.

On May 20, 1932, the county bought some nearby farm property and remodeled the house to make it suitable as a courthouse. In 1933, the renovation was complete and the county offices were relocated to that facility. That building has been expanded and remodeled several times in the years since but the outline of the original structure can still be seen.

An Illustrated History

Ford County

Organized: February 17, 1859

County Seat: Paxton

Named for: Governor of Illinois Thomas Ford

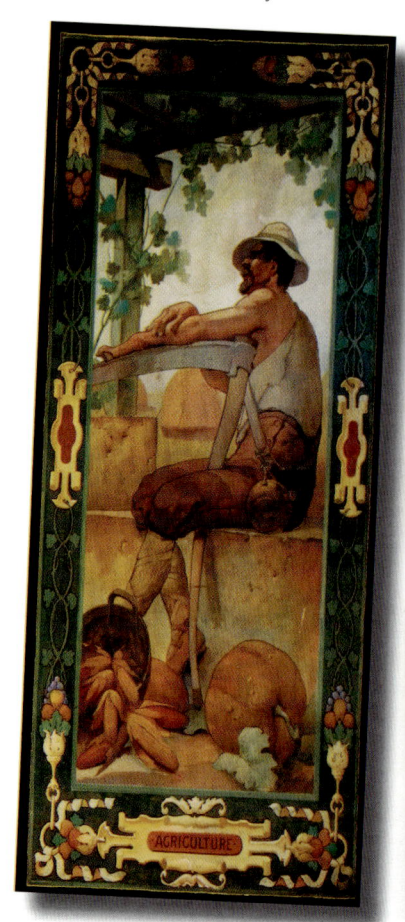

Left: Architect Joseph Royer designed the 1905 courthouse. His copper sheathed dome is unique in the state.

Inset Above: The 1862 courthouse featured a square central tower over the entrance.

Below: An anonymous itinerant artist produced the courthouse murals. The themes and style accurately represent popular public art at the turn of the twentieth century.

R. R. Murdock had a spy in the inner chambers of the state legislature. He received a confidential tip from his Springfield connection telling him where the boundaries of Ford County would be drawn before that information became public knowledge. The town of Loda was the presumptive choice to be made the county seat and the owners of that community thought they had a lock on the honor. It looked like a pat hand.

Murdock, armed with his secret information, quietly created a new town. He knew in advance that his new town, which he named Paxton, would be inside the county while Loda would find itself outside the county's boundaries.

When the map of the new county was unveiled, Paxton was positioned correctly to be selected as the county seat while the founders of Loda were left to pound sand.

The county built its first courthouse in 1862. In 1905, when talk of replacing that building began to circulate in the local newspapers, a feud blossomed between Paxton and Gibson City over moving the location of the county seat. Eighty men from Gibson City boasted of their pledge to build a new courthouse if their town was chosen. Meanwhile, Paxton's county officials said they would only renovate the 1862 building in the interest of saving taxpayers money.

The officials' promises of fiscal frugality led them to triumph on election day and Paxton retained the county seat honor. However, soon afterward, the county officials "remodeled" the old building into a pile of rubble. A new courthouse was dedicated in Paxton in 1908.

50 | Illinois Courthouses

Franklin County

Organized: January 2, 1818

County Seat: Benton

Named for: Benjamin Franklin

Above: Architect John St. Clair designed the 1875 courthouse. The one-story wings were added in the twentieth century.

Below: Charlie Birger, a cheerful outlaw, liked to pose with his gang for postcard photos. He is the man wearing a bulletproof vest and holding a machine gun. The outlaw gang's "Robin Hood" reputation ended in 1926 after Birger murdered Joseph Adams, the mayor of West City. In 1928, Charlie went to the gallows, the last man to be executed by hanging in Illinois.

Franklin County was formed while Illinois was still a federal territory. States that were not members of the original thirteen colonies were designated as a "territory" as a political precursor to statehood. It was a system in which a territorial governor and legislators got to make some of the decisions but most of the political control was still in the hands of the federal government. In 1809, the Illinois territory was carved from the Northwest Territory, the huge tract of land west of the Appalachian Mountains ceded to the United States by the British in 1783 at the end of the War of Independence.

Franklin County was created eleven months before Illinois entered into the Union as a state on December 3, 1818. The Franklin County Commissioners established a temporary seat of justice at Moses Garrett's tavern and dispatched three men to seek out a site for a permanent county seat. The committee did not travel far. Garrett evidently liked holding court in his parlor. He donated the requisite twenty acres and his land became the site of the county seat.

Frankfort was selected as the name and, after property lines and streets were platted, it was named as the county seat. Homes and businesses sprang forth around the town square and a log courthouse was erected in 1826.

In 1835, the legislature shifted Franklin County's western boundary to align with the Little Wabash River. More changes occurred in 1839 when Williamson County was established, dramatically shifting Frankfort's location from its previous central spot on the map. The old county seat now found itself situated near the county's southern border.

The legislature responded to petitions from the citizens and authorized the relocation of the county seat to a more central spot. The site selected was a piece of ground on what was then empty prairie and on January 7, 1841, the town of Benton was born. Once again a county seat was built from scratch.

Benton's first courthouse was a small frame building that burned in 1843. In 1845, that structure was replaced at a cost of $3,000 (about $68,000 in 2007).

Construction on the present courthouse was scheduled in 1870 but work was not completed until 1874 due to poor crop yields that resulted in a decline in tax revenue.

An Illustrated History | 51

Fulton County

Organized: January 28, 1823

County Seat: Lewistown

Named for: Robert Fulton, inventor of the steam engine

Left: The 1897 Fulton County Courthouse.

Inset Above: Minor changes have been made to the courthouse's entrance.

Below Top: The 1823 courthouse was a simple, hand-hewn log building.

Bottom: The 1838 courthouse was destroyed by fire in December 1894. (Artist: Floyd Lowary)

In 1821, Ossian Ross settled in Fulton County, the first white man to move into the area. Ross was a veteran of the War of 1812 and he came to Fulton County to collect his "bounty land" bonus. He staked claim to a quarter section of federal land in the part of Illinois that was still known as the Military Tract.

In 1822, Ross founded the town of Lewistown, naming it after his eldest son. The next year, Fulton County was separated from Pike County. The new county included all of the land north of the Illinois River to the Wisconsin line. It stretched eastward all the way to Lake Michigan and included the tiny army outpost known as Fort Dearborn.

In 1825, the General Assembly would carve Knox, Peoria, and Schuyler counties from Fulton County. Change was fast approaching northern Illinois as more and more white settlers began to move onto the open prairie, a land that was still untouched by plow and unencumbered by fences. These changes soon would boil up and culminate in the Black Hawk War of 1832-1833.

But, before all of that happened, the huge county existed without roads or towns. Millions of acres of vast wilderness lay under the tenuous jurisdiction of Lewistown, a tiny village that was located a few miles west of the Illinois River.

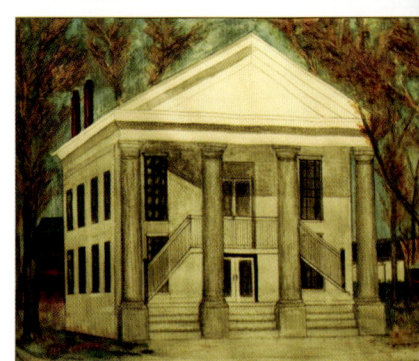

52 | Illinois Courthouses

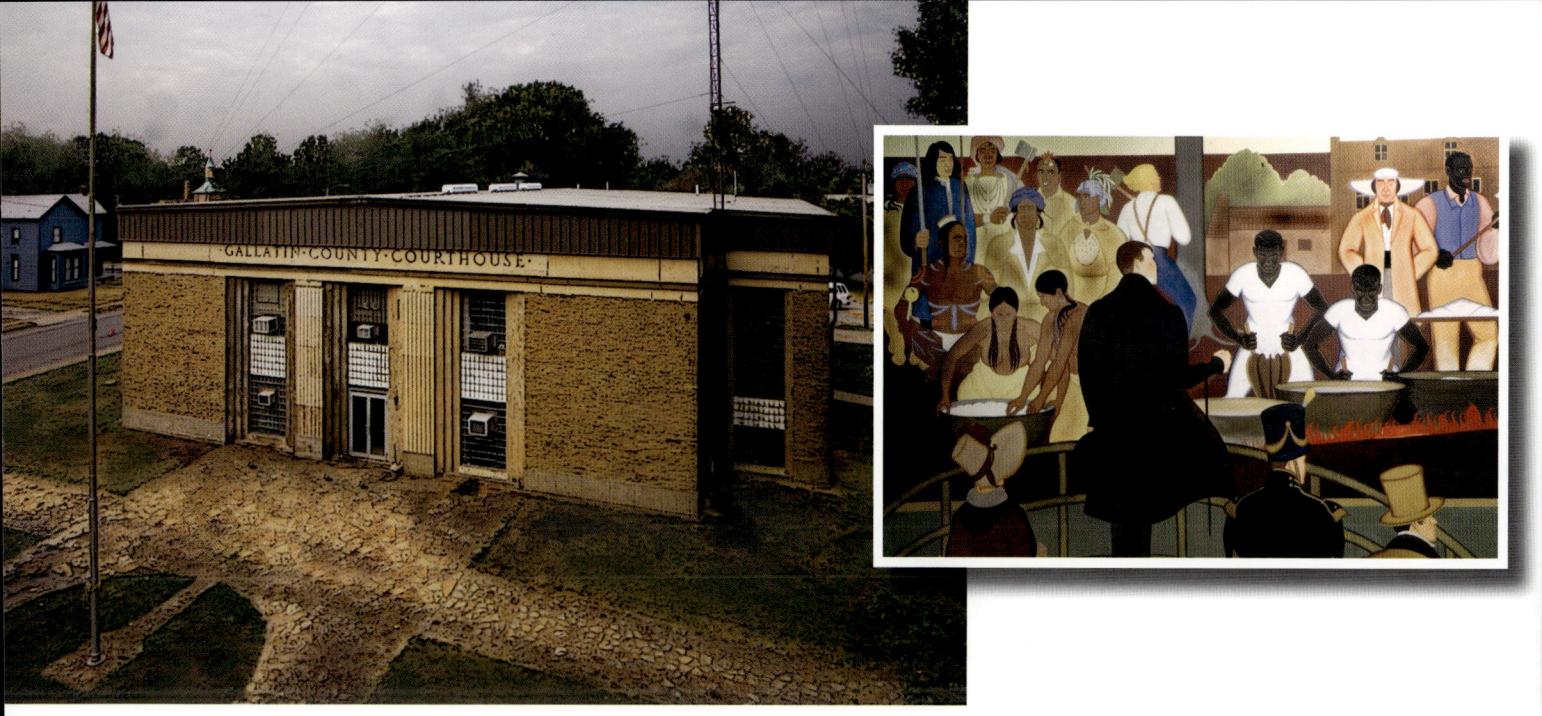

Above: Gallatin's courthouse was built in 1939 with federal assistance after the town was moved to higher ground. Courtyard bricks were reset in 2007.

Inset Above: A WPA mural covers the width of one wall in the courtroom. One section of the county's visual history depicts Native Americans and slaves boiling the saline water to make salt. Manufacturing salt was the county's principal industry until the 1870s. (Artist: Earl Ledyard, 1941)

Below: The 1857 courthouse at "Old Shawneetown" was razed after the flood of 1937. (Library of Congress: HABS photo by Russell Lee, 1939)

Gallatin County

Organized: September 14, 1812

County Seat: Shawneetown

Named for: Albert Gallatin, U.S. Secretary of the Interior

Gallatin County passed through many hands—prehistoric clans, Native Americans, the French, and the British—before it became American. It was valuable real estate to all who controlled it because it was a prolific source of salt, an essential mineral for life. The salt also attracted animals and the Saline River Valley teemed with beaver and other wildlife, making it rich hunting land.

In 1779, it was the United States' turn to take advantage of the salt resources in Gallatin County. The first treaties between the Illinois Territory and the local Native American tribes were written to insure that the crews boiling and extracting the salt would not be scalped for violating tribal hunting grounds.

Salt production in Gallatin County became a most vital industry. It had to be protected from disruption because sale of salt generated the tax revenue that supported the territory's entire budget. Salt mining and refining was such an essential industry that even though Illinois entered the Union as a "free state," the state constitution contained a loop-hole that permitted the salt-making factories to continue using slave laborers imported from plantations on the Kentucky side of the Ohio River. The exception ended in 1825.

Shawneetown was Gallatin County's original seat of justice. The town was susceptible to flooding, however, and Equality became the county seat in 1827. The honor returned to Shawneetown in 1852, but after the great Ohio River Flood of 1937, the entire town was to be moved to its present location, inland and on higher ground. "Old Shawneetown," the original site of the town, is still located on the Ohio River.

Greene County

Organized: January 20, 1821

County Seat: Carrollton

Named for: Nathaniel Greene, Revolutionary War General

The one-hundred-pound rifle on the courthouse lawn is part of a GAR memorial that was commissioned in 1901 by General William P. Carlin, a nephew of Thomas Carlin. The building's 1890 construction budget was $39,700 (about $890,000 in 2007).

The county's first courthouse was constructed in 1822. The building was on land donated by Thomas Carlin, one of the men on the site selection committee and who, in 1838, was elected as the sixth governor of Illinois. The courthouse square had three whipping posts to ensure that the guilty would not be kept waiting. The prompt punishment of horse thieves and scofflaws was considered more humane than forcing them to spend days and nights locked in stocks exposed to angry citizens, cruel children, and the elements.

Top: William and Thomas Finley constructed the 1822 frame courthouse. On the right is a stray pen used for lost and found animals. (Artwork: original black and white sketch by Vi Sullivan, color enhanced)

Bottom: Thomas Rattan constructed the 1830 courthouse. That building was 44 by 46 feet. The courtroom and several offices were on the first floor and the top floor was one large room for public gatherings and two small rooms for petit juries. An annex was added in 1883.

In 1830, contractor Thomas Rattan built a brick courthouse. He topped the building's spire with a shiny tin ball, about two feet in diameter that had been imported from St. Louis, Missouri. The ball is remembered because of a story about a woodpecker that made a habit of pecking on it. The bird's incessant tap-tap-tap shattered the peace throughout the building but especially in the courtroom. One day the judge stopped court, grabbed his rifle, and ran outside. He had murder in his eye and was determined to blast the bird to kingdom come. The tin ball got the worst of it, receiving several bullet holes, and the bird flew off unscathed. The building was expanded in 1883 with the addition of fire resistant vaults and offices.

In 1891, architect Henry Elliot designed the present courthouse which was completed in 1892. A clock was added in 1893. The steps leading up to the covered porch are red granite.

Grundy County

Organized: February 17, 1841

County Seat: Morris

Named for: Felix Grundy, U.S. Attorney General

The Illinois and Michigan (I and M) Canal runs through the heart of Grundy County. During the 1830s and 1840s that ninety-six-mile-long waterway pulsed with commercial vitality. Construction of the canal was one of Illinois' most ambitious internal development projects—it connected Lake Michigan with the Mississippi River and enabled water transportation from the Great Lakes all the way south to the Gulf of Mexico. It was Illinois' answer to the fabled Erie Canal.

Once committed to the project, the state supported the canal legislatively at every turn. The act authorizing the establishment of Grundy County even stipulated that the county seat had to be located on land adjacent to the canal and on canal property. The rule of placing the county seat near the geographic center of the county was overlooked while nervous legislators did everything they could to insure the success of the canal. Three of the six commissioners appointed to decide where to locate the Grundy County seat openly represented the canal's interests. The county seat was named after Isaac Morris, one of those commissioners.

The first courthouse in Morris, a frame building, was constructed in 1842. That building was replaced in 1856 by a brick courthouse of some size and architectural assurance. The current courthouse, completed in 1913, occupies the same site as the first two courthouses.

The canal declined in importance during the 1850s when railroads became the premier freight haulers in Illinois. The now-quiet I and M Canal has been preserved as a National Historic Site.

Above: An old "Indian pole" grave marker stands on the courthouse lawn. The pole stood for many years near the tow path of Illinois and Michigan Canal, marking the grave of Nucquette, a chief of the Potawatomie Tribe. It was moved to the courthouse lawn in 1925.

Above Left: The 1912 courthouse was designed by architect Joseph Royer. Restoration work in 2000 was supervised by architect John Garrett.

Left: Art Ashcraft, courthouse maintenance worker, painted the murals that cover several walls in the recorder's office. The murals depict some of the area's historic buildings. The two-story building with a dome is the 1856 courthouse.

56 | Illinois Courthouses

Top Right: The 1938 courthouse is one of Illinois' few WPA courthouses.

Inset: A proposal surfaced in 1900, but the courthouse was never built.

Below Top: Members of the site selection committee carved a "C" on a black oak tree to mark the center of the new county seat. (Artist: Ralph Harrelson)

Below Bottom: The 1840 courthouse burned in 1894.

Hamilton County

Organized: February 8, 1821

County Seat: McLeansboro

Named for: Alexander Hamilton

Hamilton County was part of White County before 1821. After legislators authorized the establishment of the county, commissioners were sent into the woods to find a site for the county seat as near to the geographic center of the county as possible.

They walked to a twenty acre piece of land that had been donated to the county by William McLean, a local physician and land speculator. In order to find the center of the heavily wooded site, they separated and went to three different spots on the parameter of the property. At an agreed upon time, they each walked in a straight line into the dense woods. When they met, they figured that point was the approximate center of the track. They marked the spot by cutting the letter "C" in the trunk of a black oak tree. That tree marked the center of the town square for the new county seat.

McLean donated another twenty acres to the county on the condition that he receive one third of the profits from the sale of the land and that the county seat would be named in his honor. Thus, the name is McLeansboro.

Early court sessions were held at the house of John Anderson. The first courthouse was a hewn-log structure, 16 by 16 foot square, with a plank floor. The building had one window, with glass panes, and a three-foot-wide plank door.

In 1840, the county built a brick courthouse. The contractor was Isaac Laswell. That building was destroyed by fire in 1894.

Forty-four years passed before the county built another courthouse. A jail and "fireproof" building for storage of records were built on the site of the former courthouse, but court sessions and administrative duties of the county were conducted from "court quarters," rented rooms that were located on the south side of the square. The idea of building a new courthouse was floated in 1900. Proponents circulated an architect's rendering to stir up interest, but the project withered due to lack of support.

The county built its current courthouse in 1938. It was a WPA grant project and William R. McCoy was the architect.

State Capitals of Illinois

In the years since Illinois was admitted into the Union, the state capital has been established in three different cities and the General Assembly has met in six statehouses. Two of the old statehouse buildings were transformed into county courthouses after their service as capitols was over.

The town of Kaskaskia was Illinois' first capital city. It was located near where the Kaskaskia River flows into the Mississippi River. In 1703 the Jesuits founded a mission there. The French built Fort Kaskaskia in 1733. The British gained control during the French and Indian War and it passed into American hands in 1778 when George Rogers Clark defeated the English in the area and it became part of the Northwest Territory. From 1809 to 1818, Kaskaskia was capital of the Illinois Territory.

In 1818, Illinois was admitted into the union and the territorial capital automatically became Illinois' first state capital. The General Assembly met in a simple, two-story brick building that was rented for $122 a month (about $2,050 in 2007). The twenty-nine members of the House of Representatives met on the first floor while the state's fourteen senators met on the floor above. The Mississippi River has meandered during the nineteenth century and Kaskaskia is on land on the Missouri side of the river.

Left: The Kaskaskia statehouse was a rented building. The town was the territorial capital from 1809 to 1818. After statehood was achieved, Kaskaskia served as the state capital for one year before the capital was transferred to Vandalia. The building was destroyed by flooding, probably around 1844. (Library of Congress, HABS section, DN-0063723, Chicago Daily News negatives collection, Chicago History Museum)

Right: This historic statehouse was the third one built at Vandalia. It was erected in 1836 and little used by the legislature since they voted to move to Springfield early in 1837.

Inset Below: The building was renovated as a state historic site in 1933. State officials occupied large office spaces on the first floor. The state senate and representatives met in their respective rooms (chambers) on the second floor. Some state officers were housed in separate buildings.

The state government met at Kaskaskia for only two years and then relocated in 1820. Vandalia was selected as the new capital city. No site north of the Kaskaskia River was given serious consideration at the time because only the southern one-third of the state was inhabited to a notable degree with white settlers. The upper two-thirds of Illinois was under the control of Native American tribes.

There were three statehouses built at Vandalia. The first was a plain, two-story frame building. It was destroyed by fire and rebuilt in 1824 at a cost of $15,000 (about $369,000 in 2007).

At about the same time as the second statehouse was opened for business at Vandalia, settlers began moving into the northern regions of the state in greater numbers. Members of the General Assembly began discussing the idea of moving the capital to a more central location. In 1833, legislators passed enabling legislation that would allow voters to choose between the cities of Vandalia, Jacksonville, Peoria, Springfield, or Alton.

Vandalia's town leaders, who previously had demonstrated a languorous attitude toward hosting the state's legislators, sprang into action. In 1836, while the General Assembly was in recess, they tore down the drab old state capitol and replaced it with a new brick statehouse. The replacement building cost the city $16,000 (about $337,500 in 2007).

An Illustrated History | 59

Left: The old state capitol at Springfield is now a historic site. It was used as the Sangamon County Courthouse for many years.

Inset Above: Lincoln's chair in the old Hall of Representatives is draped in black. His top hat remains on his desk, perhaps signifying his abrupt departure.

Left: The 1888 statehouse is a fine example of the neo-classical architectural influences of the age.

Inset Above: In 1986, the magnificent dome above the capitol rotunda was restored to its 1888 brilliance.

Right: Work began on the old Springfield statehouse, a Greek Revival-style building, in 1837. The original building had two stories and a basement. In 1899, the building was raised and a third floor was inserted at ground level. In 1961 the building was designated a National Historic Landmark and in 1966 was listed on the National Register of Historic Places. (Library of Congress - Historic American Buildings Survey)

The grand gesture was too little, too late. In 1837, the legislators voted to move the state capital to Springfield. The cornerstone was laid that July 4th, but the legislature continued to meet in Vandalia for the next two years while construction of a new statehouse was underway in Springfield. Ironically, the old Sangamon County Courthouse had to be razed first to make room for the new statehouse. The old Vandalia building was given to Fayette County to be used as a courthouse. In 1933, it was purchased by the state and restored as a historic site.

In 1839, some portions of the fifth capitol were opened, but another fifteen years would pass before work on the building was completed. The building, designed by architect John P. Hague, cost $240,000 (about $4,866,000 in 2007). Springfield had agreed to provide $50,000 but when the city found it impossible to raise the final one-third of its pledge, one hundred citizens, including Abraham Lincoln, signed a note to cover this expense. This statehouse is the one most closely associated with Abraham Lincoln's years in Springfield. It is the building where he was laid in state before burial at Oak Ridge Cemetery.

In 1876, the state decided to build yet another statehouse. The old building was turned over to Sangamon County to be used as a courthouse. In 1899, the building was jacked up and a ground floor was inserted, the upper floors remaining essentially unchanged except the Hall of Representatives was changed to accommodate the circuit court. This renovation was considered one of the great engineering feats of the age. Like the Vandalia building, this statehouse was reclaimed by the state and restored as a historical site. During the 1960s, it was completely dismantled and rebuilt.

The sixth and present capitol was completed in 1888. It was designed by architects John Cochrane, George Garnsey, and Alfred Piquenard, who also were active in designing county courthouses and other notable buildings throughout Illinois.

Hancock County

Organized: January 13, 1825

County Seat: Carthage

Named for: John Hancock

In 1825, Montebello, a Mississippi River town on the western edge of the county, was selected as a temporary county seat. Citizens living inland soon grew weary of traveling to the town's inconvenient location and they petitioned legislators for a county seat positioned at a more centrally-located site. In 1833, the legislature acquiesced and authorized the founding of Carthage as the new permanent county seat. The county built a hewn-log building to house the court and, in 1839, a second, more substantial courthouse was built.

In 1858, during their contest for an Illinois Senate seat, Abraham Lincoln and Stephen A. Douglas both spoke at the 1839 courthouse, but on different days. Douglas, a Democrat, always was a Hancock County "favorite son" and he received the majority of votes from the county residents in every race he entered. In 1860, the county's voters again cast their votes for him when he ran against Abraham Lincoln for the presidency.

Moses Stephens built the 1839 courthouse for a fee of $3,700 (about $74,900 in 2007) and it served the community until 1906 when it was razed to make room for a new courthouse.

As was frequently the case when county officials announced that they were contemplating building a new courthouse, other towns would begin maneuvering to become the new county seat. That was exactly what occurred in Hancock County. The town of Warsaw sought to become the new county seat, but Carthage prevailed when the question was placed before the voters. The present courthouse was dedicated on October 21, 1908. Joseph E. Mills was the architect.

Above: The statue of Lady Justice that stands atop the dome looked down on six thousand elementary school children who assembled at the courthouse in 1925 to commemorate the centennial anniversary of the founding of Hancock County.

Inset Above: A colorful stained glass version of Lady Justice overlooks the twin stairs at the courtroom level of the courthouse.

62 | Illinois Courthouses

Hardin County

Organized: March 2, 1839

County Seat: Elizabethtown

Named for: Hardin County, Kentucky

Above: When the courthouse opened, a single-face clock was installed in the round window at the roof line. In 1928, a tower was added to the building and a multi-faced clock was installed. Both clocks were donated by Josie Fowler in honor of her late husband Dr. F. M. Fowler.

Below: Photographs indicate that the 1889 building, and the one it replaced, were nearly identical. Courthouse fires have destroyed most of the county's old records.

Information about Hardin County's first courthouse was lost in a fire that consumed the county's second courthouse. The blaze occurred on May 19, 1884. Ironically the courthouse that burned, a brick building, was supposed to be a more fire resistant building than the one it replaced, a frame structure.

A new courthouse was built five years later, in 1889. The contractor used the same plans that had been used to construct the building that burned in 1884, so, for all practical purposes, the two buildings were identical.

In a tragic déjà vu, that building burned on December 2, 1921, destroying even more of the already sparse county records. Researching the county's early history continues to be problematic.

To rebuild once again, the voters went to the polls on April 13, 1926, and voted "yes" to an indebtedness of $20,000 (about $197,500 in 2007). That is all they thought they could afford to pay for a new courthouse. The depression that hit the rest of the country a few years later had already arrived in Hardin County. Architect Thomas S. Thompson submitted his plan for the building, but all the bids from contractors had to be rejected as being too high. The lowest bid was $34,845 (about $344,100 in 2007).

George Corder, a local contractor, saved the day. He agreed to work for a daily fee of $12 (about $475 in 2007), plus materials. The total cost of the project is not readily available, but if Corder worked six days a week, resting only on Sundays, during the year that it took him to build the courthouse, his labor would have cost the county only $3,744. The cost of material and salary for several assistants would have added to the expense, but it was still a great bargain for the county.

The courthouse was dedicated on July 30 and 31, 1927. The dedication ceremony had to be spread over two days because on day one, Saturday, the 30th, a gully-washing thunderstorm sent the dignitaries running for cover midway through the program. Undaunted, the fifty-member school band from Harrisburg reassembled on the lawn the next morning and restarted the ceremony. By noon on Sunday, the 31st, speeches and ribbon cutting had been completed to the satisfaction of all.

Henderson County

Organized: January 20, 1841

County Seat: Oquawka

Named for: Henderson County, Kentucky

Left: The Henderson County Courthouse dates from 1842. The building was renovated in 1965 using plans that had been drafted in 1946 by the architectural firm of Scribbins, Klusmeyer and Mears.

Middle: The 1842 courthouse was built by Alexis Phelps, the man who donated land to help found Oquawka. (Library of Congress, HABS section)

Below: Henderson County Clerk Marcella Cisna displays an antique jurist chair. The springs fastened to the front legs allowed a jury member to rock away long hours in court.

The Henderson County Commissioners held their first meeting on Monday, April 19, 1841. Later that week, on Thursday, Alexis Phelps, one of the county commissioners, donated two hundred surveyed lots to the county to help create the town of Oquawka. The donated real estate was auctioned to pay for public buildings.

In 1842, when the county treasury was flush enough to pay bills, the commissioners took bids from contractors to build a courthouse. Phelps, the county's benefactor, recouped some of his donation when he was chosen to build the courthouse. His was the low bid: $1,219 (about $26,800 in 2007). One assumes that Phelps's winning bid and commissionership were merely coincidental.

Phelps hired several sub-contractors to do the actual work. James Ryason was hired to furnish 175,000 bricks and the stone, windows, and doors for the new building. Two men, Woodworth and Merrill, built the foundation, walls, and roof. The team worked well together and the building was completed quickly.

Stephen A. Douglas, still in the circuit judge phase of his brilliant Illinois legal and political career, presided over court sessions at this courthouse until November 1843. Two fire-resistant vaults were added in later years, but a major remodeling plan was defeated in 1946 by the voters and renovations to the building were shelved until 1965.

Henry County

Organized: January 13, 1825

County Seat: Cambridge

Named for: Patrick Henry

Above Middle: The 1866 courthouse has been remodeled several times. An annex was added in 1940.

Above Left: Henry County has one of the most colorful courtrooms in Illinois. It was redecorated in 1950. The firm of Buckles & Milani directed a third-floor remodel in 1968. Italo J. Milani, architect, supervised a second-floor remodel in 1969. The 1998 judicial wing installation was designed by Phillips, Swager & Associates and Legat Architects, Incorporated.

The Brandenburg Tavern at Dayton was the temporary county seat from 1837 until 1839. The ale house was the only building in the area with sufficient room where a crowd might gather to watch the court in action. There were those with a more cynical bent who suggested that the availability of adult beverages played more of a role. Quaffing a liabation was a popular custom on the frontier after a jury reached a favorable, or unfavorable, decision.

A courthouse was built at Richmond in 1838 but a mysterious fire destroyed that building after only one month.

The county seat was moved to Morristown. It was not centrally located, but the town's owners outbid other contenders with an offer of 160 acres, 16 lots, and $1,000 (about $20,000 in 2007). Legislators and county officials accepted the attractive offer. The citizens who had to travel an inconveniently long distance to reach the county seat thought otherwise. Despite their objections, work began on a courthouse at Morristown.

Geneseo, for some reason, was named as the temporary county seat while the Morristown courthouse was being built. The courthouse at Morristown opened in 1841 but the discontent about the inconvenient location had not abated. Eventually, legislators were forced to respond to petitions to move the county seat.

The town of Sugar Tree Grove (later renamed Cambridge) was selected as the new county seat but Morristown was reluctant to surrender its claim on the honor and refused to transfer its set of county records. In 1843, Cambridge's citizens took the matter into their own hands. They hoisted the courthouse onto runners and hitched a team of seventy oxen to the sled. They lugged the courthouse twelve miles to its new home at Cambridge.

In 1845, a new courthouse was built at Cambridge and that building was used for more than thirty years. The present courthouse was started in 1866 and construction on the building continued over the next twelve years until it was completed in 1880.

Iroquois County

Organized: February 26, 1833

County Seat: Watseka

Named for: The Iroquois Confederation of Native American Tribes

Katherine Grace Clifton, a shy heiress with the moxie to pilot her own plane, died in 1961 at age sixty-seven. She bequeathed one-third of her five million dollar fortune to Iroquois County to build a new courthouse at Watseka. The courthouse was dedicated in 1966.

Clifton did not explain her motive for including the generous donation in her will, but most believe that she only wished to benefit the people with whom she had lived and worked all of her life.

C. W. Raymond, Clifton's stepfather and a former federal judge, was the man who built up the family's wealth. Throughout the 1890s, Raymond bought up poorer quality farmland that no one else wanted to mess with. He studiously upgraded the sandy soil by adding fertilizer and chemicals. The value of his holdings rose proportionally. By the time he passed away in 1939, Raymond had twenty-seven farms in his portfolio. Katherine took over active management of the farms after he died.

Left: The architectural firm of Graham, Anderson, Probst & White designed the 1966 courthouse. The building was constructed on land that Clifton's husband had purchased to be used as a municipal airport.

Inset Above: Katherine Clifton's donation is a rare example on a single individual underwriting the construction of a new courthouse.

In 1940, the Watseka heiress took an interest in flying. She also took an interest in her flight instructor, William Clifton, and the two were married. Clifton died in 1957, but Katherine continued making daily flights over her extensive holdings, keeping track of crops, drainage problems, and all of the details involved with managing such far flung holdings. She remained an avid aviatrix, taking friends for aerial jaunts to Chicago and other destinations. In her later years it was a familiar sight to see her enjoying a cup of coffee at her favorite hamburger joint, still dressed in her flying gear. She is remembered as a swell dame who left a nice tip on the counter for her friends as she went out the door.

In 1835, some land speculators donated twenty acres to Iroquois County on the condition that the county seat would be established there. The site was called Iroquois but it was a "paper" town that existed only as notations in a surveyor's field book at that point. The deal was struck but for some reason Iroquois never materialized. The county's business was conducted from rented rooms in Montgomery. The county residents allowed this state of affairs to stand for awhile but Montgomery was far from the center of the county and it was never an acceptable choice. Eventually, citizens took action and petitioned for a change. In 1839, the state legislature authorized the transfer of the county seat from Montgomery to Middleport. A courthouse was built there in 1843.

In 1858, the Peoria and Oquawka Railroad was building a rail line that would run from Peoria to the Indiana state line. The tracks were to pass through the county seat but the plan came unhinged when the city fathers baulked at donating land for a depot.

The dispute opened the door for men who owned land a short distance southeast of the county seat. They arranged a quid pro quo with the Peoria and Oquawka Railroad and, presto, the route detoured a mile south of Middleport. A new town was born, called South Middleport (the name was changed to Watseka in 1865). "Old" Middleport was absorbed into Watseka as that town expanded.

In 1865, commissioners decided to abandon the old courthouse at Middleport and built a new one at Watseka. The county rented space to hold court and conduct business while the new courthouse was being built. Soon after it was finished, on October 16, 1866, that building burned and many of the county's records were lost. Some speculated that the mysterious blaze was retaliation for abandoning the Middleport courthouse.

The structure was rebuilt and additions were made in 1881 and 1927. The building was decommissioned in 1966 and is now a museum.

Top: Architect C. B. Leach designed the 1866 courthouse. His fee was $300 ($3,940 in 2007). The courthouse was expanded in 1881 and 1927; the top of the dome was altered several times before the building was donated to the Iroquois County Historical Society for use as a museum in 1967.

Bottom: The 1843 courthouse at Middleport was abandoned in 1865 when the county seat was shifted to nearby Watseka.

Jackson County

Organized: January 10, 1816

County Seat: Murphysboro

Named for: Andrew Jackson, the hero of the Battle of New Orleans

Jackson County is one of the several southern Illinois counties that make up "Little Egypt." The name came from the area's similarity with the Nile River delta. The annual spring flooding of the Mississippi River enhanced the comparison.

The town of Brownville, located on the banks of the Big Muddy River, was Jackson County's first county seat. A courthouse was constructed there but the town's river location was never popular for the county's residents, most of whom lived farther inland. The issue led to frequent requests to have the county seat moved to a more centrally-located site. The people's dissatisfaction became more pronounced after a fire destroyed the courthouse and it became obvious that a new building would have to be erected anyway.

In 1843, the General Assembly authorized a search for a new site. The site selection committee tagged Murphysboro, a town ironically situated only a few miles upstream from the first county seat. The move was made and Brownville languished until it eventually disappeared.

In 1846, the county built a brick courthouse and jail at Murphysboro. The Pauley Company designed the building. Pauley was a blacksmith who started out repairing boilers and iron fittings on riverboats. Eventually, he got into the business of building iron cages that were bolted on wagons and used for transporting prisoners. That work led to an association with courthouses and jail keepers. After his son studied a little structural engineering, Pauley expanded into building jail houses. In due time, the former blacksmith and his son added the design and construction of courthouses to their repertoire.

Three hangings were held at the 1846 courthouse between 1895 and 1915. That building was razed on June 1, 1927, to clear the way for the present courthouse. The 1927 courthouse was designed by N. S. Spencer and Son, another father and son architectural firm.

Above: The 1927 courthouse is an example of turn-of-the-century classicism. This architectural style retains traces of Romanesque and Greek-Revival elements but on the whole represents a clear shift toward more streamlined, businesslike, modern designs.

Below: In 1898, a jail was built at the rear of the old 1846 courthouse. The contractor got his start in the prison industry by building wagons with iron cages that were used to transport prisoners.

68 | Illinois Courthouses

Right: Some time in the twentieth century the tower from the 1876 courthouse was removed and the roof altered.

Inset Above: The 1876 courthouse original design included a central tower and portico.

Jasper County

Organized: February 15, 1831

County Seat: Newton

Named for: William Jasper, Revolutionary Army soldier

In 1831, Louis W. Jordan held title to the land at the geographic center of the newly formed Jasper County. Jordan, one of the first white settlers in the area, donated twenty acres of that land so a county seat could be built there. His generosity increased the value of his other land holdings and may have aided his political career to boot. He was elected as the sheriff of the newly organized county.

As aficionados of western lore know, frontier justice tended to be straightforward and quick. During the 1830s, the Illinois prairie was the "wild west" and the lawmen of the age considered a stranger suspect. The application of justice was not always evenhanded.

Such on-the-spot justice created controversy. One person who experienced Jordan's brand of "street justice" claimed that the sheriff abused his authority and "terrorized" innocent citizens. Other reports from that time praised the sheriff's aggressiveness when it was necessary to control drunks, ruffians, and scofflaws who disturbed the public peace.

Meeting minutes dated March 1835 provide the first mention of building a courthouse, a hewn-log structure. Some meetings also were held at Sheriff Jordan's house.

In 1839, a second courthouse was built. It was a forty-foot-square, two-story, brick building. The construction work was done by Benjamin Harris, but records indicated that the work on the building was only partially completed. Even so, the county accepted the structure in 1841 and Harris was paid $2,875 (about $60,000 in 2007). It is not clear why the commissioners considered the building unfinished. It served the county for the next thirty-five years.

In 1876, construction began on the county's present courthouse. The builders' contract was awarded to J. I. LaGrange and Charles Eppinghouser for $34,165 (about $639,000 in 2007).

The outer appearance of this building remains relatively unchanged, but the central tower has been removed and the pitched roof lowered. Unfortunately, the remodeling of the building also involved removal of the pediment from above the main entrance.

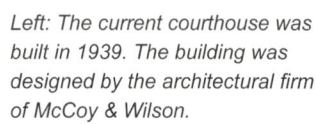

Left: The current courthouse was built in 1939. The building was designed by the architectural firm of McCoy & Wilson.

Inset Above: The 1871 courthouse was destroyed by a tornado. The American Red Cross, the organization that Clara Barton had founded just seven years earlier in 1881, was one of the organizations that rushed to the aid of the injured and displaced. (Artist: Robert Trout)

Jefferson County

Organized: March 26, 1819

County Seat: Mount Vernon

Named for: Thomas Jefferson

During September 1819, contractor John Sanders built the county's first courthouse. He was paid $85 (about $1,740 in 2007). The hewn-log, 18 by 20 foot, one-story building was close-fitted enough to shelter the court during the warm days of summer but its ability to keep out the weather left much to be desired when the winds of late autumn started blowing through the cracks. The court ordered additional chinking and daubing to seal up the gaps between the logs. They also decided that adding a fireplace would be a good idea. Those improvements cost the county another $75, nearly doubling the cost of the building.

The early state law dealing with establishing a new county seat specified that three structures needed to be built as quickly as possible. The first two were well known: a courthouse and a jail. The third, now esoteric to most people, was a stray pound.

Top: The 1819 courthouse included a corral for holding stray livestock. (Artist: Robert Trout)

Bottom: The county's second courthouse was completed in 1840, but the contractor had to wait several years before being paid. (Artist: Robert Trout)

The stray pound was a corral on the town square big enough to hold a few horses, cows, and livestock that strayed from their owner's property. Pioneers rarely fenced their pasture land and trusted that "Ol' Bossie" would turn up at the stray pound if she wandered off. Communities still maintain stray pounds for the same purpose but dogs and cats are more typical clients "rescued" by these facilities today.

In 1839, one of the walls of the 1819 courthouse collapsed. The county court ordered the construction of a new brick courthouse. William Edwards was hired to build a forty by forty foot building with a cupola and he was supposed to be paid $5,500 (about $111,000 in 2007). He completed the building in 1840 but, unfortunately for Edwards, all he got when he presented his bill was an I.O.U. from the county treasurer. Tax revenue had declined and it was several years before Edwards was fully recompensed.

In 1871, architect R. Rose designed the county's third courthouse. Sadly, that building was totally destroyed on February 19, 1888, when a tornado roared through the heart of Mount Vernon, destroying most of the town's buildings. Thirty-seven people died and hundreds more were injured by the storm. Assistance and aid poured into Mount Vernon from nearly every state and territory in the Union. In 1889, the courthouse was rebuilt under the guidance of architect J. W. Gaddis.

The current courthouse was built in 1939, one of only six Illinois courthouses built during the WPA era.

An Illustrated History

Jersey County

Organized: February 28, 1839

County Seat: Jerseyville

Named for: State of New Jersey

Above Left: The 1893 courthouse was designed by Henry Elliott, a Chicago architect.

Above Right: Deputy Bill Bridges stands in the courthouse entrance hall. Bridges served as chief of police for the city before assuming his security duties at the courthouse.

A surveyor platted Jerseyville's property lines and right-of-ways in 1834. The town was chartered in 1837 and it was fully incorporated as a city in 1867. The origin of the town's name is vague, but one story is that many of the first settlers came from New Jersey and wanted to remember their home state. Another version is that John Lott, the landowner who ordered the survey, got tired of listening to different names being suggested and decided upon Jerseyville to end the debate.

The first courthouse was built in 1840. Peyton Walker and Aaron Rue handled the carpentry on the building and Peter Perrine did the brick work. The court's original order called for the builders to put up an eighteen foot square structure, but change orders were issued and the finished structure was a forty by forty foot square building. In 1862, a sixteen by thirty foot jail was attached to the courthouse.

In January 1884, the courthouse caught fire. A defective flue started the blaze after the building had been closed for the day and, unfortunately, by the time the alarm was raised, four prisoners had died from smoke inhalation. The county rebuilt the jail almost immediately but replacing the courthouse was delayed for several years due to a depressed economy.

The cornerstone for the present courthouse was dedicated in 1893.

Right: A street front view of the 1839 courthouse.

Inset Above: After two additions, the courthouse now stretches for nearly a block.

Below: The building was capped with a tower and mansard roof in 1900. The tower was damaged and removed during the 1930s.

Jo Daviess County

Organized: February 17, 1827

County Seat: Galena

Named for: Joseph (Jo) Daviess, killed at the Battle of Tippecanoe

The federal government never surrendered its mining rights to the rich deposits of lead and zinc ore that laced the hills around Galena. So, when the state authorized the establishment of Jo Daviess County, the county officials had no public land that they could auction to raise money to build public buildings. Ironically, the county seat straddled the most abundant mineral deposits in the state but could not afford to build a courthouse. Meanwhile, the ore mining industry drew hundreds of workers and their families to the area every week.

County offices were housed in rented rooms around the town square. Elected officials conducted business on the fly and stored important papers in their tall stovepipe hats, a habit which Abe Lincoln was prone to as a state representative and lawyer.

In 1838, the county decided it was time to put up a courthouse and a contest was announced to see who could draw the best set of plans for a new building. Charles Rogers won the $100 prize (about $2,300 in 2007). The next year, 1839, the county hired John Slaymaker and Father Samuel Mazzuchelli, a Catholic priest, to build a courthouse using Rogers's plans. Progress was slow and it was the early months of 1845 before the court could use the building.

In July 1900, the courthouse was remodeled. This included the addition of a three-story, brick annex with mansard roof and a substantial bell tower. The tower was damaged during a storm in the 1930s and removed. Another addition was added in 1970 at the rear of the core building. The building was elongated again in 1976 when a public safety annex was added.

The 1871 courthouse is one of the oldest in continuous use in Illinois.

Johnson County

Organized: September 14, 1812

County Seat: Vienna

Named for: Richard Mentor Johnson, the man who killed Tecumseh

Ninian Edwards, the territorial governor, proclaimed Johnson County into existence with a stroke of his quill pen. That was the last time a county in Illinois could be established solely by a governor's proclamation. After 1812, the territorial legislature had to pass enabling legislation in order to establish a new county.

For the first two years of the county's existence, the temporary county seat was at the home of John Bradshaw. In 1814, the legislators appointed three commissioners to seek a site for a county seat that would be closer to the geographic center of the county. The committee duly reported their recommendation to the General Assembly but two years slipped by without further action on the matter. The county tried to jumpstart the process and hired a surveyor to lay out township lines and sections for a county seat at Lanesville (later renamed Elvira). It is unclear, but doubtful, that a courthouse was ever constructed in Elvira. It hardly mattered because in 1818 the legislators shifted the county seat to Vienna where it has remained thereafter.

A rough courthouse was quickly built at Vienna. George Brazel was the low bidder. He constructed a twenty-four by fourteen foot, hewn-log courthouse, with a partition that divided the courtroom from the jury room. Improvements, including laying wood planks on the dirt floor, followed in 1819.

A two-story, brick courthouse was erected around 1848—perhaps as early as 1839. That building was razed after the present courthouse was authorized in 1868. Joseph Frick was the low bidder and won the contract to build the structure. The next year he sold the contract for one dollar to Charles Ham and Isaac Pearce. The contract price and specification were not altered by this transaction and the two new builders completed the work in 1871.

Neal Watkins, circuit clerk, examines the bracing inside the building's clock tower.

74 | Illinois Courthouses

Temple Burned, Temple Rebuilt

In the months following the bloody 1838 "Mormon War" that was waged in Caldwell County, Missouri, Joseph Smith's followers fled across the Mississippi River into Illinois. The Missouri Militia's battle against civilians attracted nationwide attention. Smith escaped captivity in Missouri and traveled to Washington, D.C., to seek compensation and publicity.

Smith was able to meet with President Van Buren but his complaints were generally ignored at the federal level. Meanwhile, his followers found refuge at a settlement they called Nauvoo. It was located in Hancock County.

Perhaps because of the favorable press that Smith received back East, Illinois proved to be hospitable to the Mormons. The Illinois General Assembly granted Smith's followers a liberal town charter, allowing them to operate their settlement almost totally under local control.

A new Nauvoo temple opened in 2002. Thousands of tourists and church members visit the town annually to tour the region and participate in historic pageants and reenactments.

An Illustrated History | 75

Left: The 1841 Nauvoo temple shortly before it was destroyed. (Library of Congress, American Memory Section, photo by C. W. Carter, circa 1846)

Below: Joseph, Hyrum, and Emma Smith are buried near Joseph's home at Nauvoo.

Nauvoo blossomed into the largest city in Illinois and the tenth largest in the United States in only three years. The town's fame spread as the industrious Mormons built their schools, homes, and shops. A magnificent white temple sat atop a nearby bluff overlooking the town and the river valley.

But, even as Nauvoo was growing in population and the church gained political strength, trouble with non-church county authorities and internal strife about church doctrine festered just below the surface. The friction erupted in bloodshed in 1844 when a newspaper office at Nauvoo was ransacked after the editor printed stories about the alleged misconduct of the leaders of the church. Joseph Smith and his brother Hyrum were arrested and taken to the Carthage jail to await trial for their participation in the attack.

76 | Illinois Courthouses

Right: A mob stormed the Carthage jail in 1844 and officers were unable to protect the Smith brothers. The Mormon Church maintains the property as a historic site. It attracts thousands of visitors each year.

Below: The Mansion House at Nauvoo was built in 1842 as a home for Joseph Smith and his family. It later was used as a hotel to house visitors to the community. After Smith's death his widow, Emma, resided there for a number of years. (Historic American Buildings Survey – Library of Congress. Photo by Albert J. Delong, 1934.)

    Governor Thomas Ford had promised protection to the Smith brothers, but a mob attacked the jail. The Mormon leaders were armed and fought for their lives but they were overwhelmed by the mob and assassinated. The violence spread to Nauvoo. Eventually, the temple was burned. Fearing that once again the government would not protect them, the Mormons decided their best option was to evacuate the city entirely. In 1846, most of the members followed Brigham Young on the epic trek west that took them to Salt Lake City. At the time, Utah was still part of Mexico and outside the jurisdiction of the United States.

    Hyrum and Joseph Smith were buried at Nauvoo. Joseph's wife, Emma, was buried along side the brothers after she died in 1879.

    In 1999, the Mormons broke ground for a temple on the site of the original Nauvoo structure. The new building was dedicated in June 2002.

An Illustrated History | 77

Left: A green patina coats the copper covered dome of the 1892 courthouse. The soldiers and sailors memorial near the front entrance is a tribute to citizen soldiers who died in the Mexican, Civil, and Spanish Wars. It was dedicated on June 17, 1915.

Inset Above: The Justice Center in St. Charles was opened in 1993.

Kane County

Organized: January 16, 1836

County Seat: Geneva

Named for: Elias Kane, U.S. Senator from Illinois

Six months after the legislature authorized Kane County into existence, two hundred men elbowed into Herrington's Tavern at Geneva. They elected county officials and then adjourned to the lawn outside to toast the creation of their new county.

For the next few months, court sessions were held at Herrington's Tavern. In 1837, the first courthouse was constructed. It stood at what is now the corner of 4th and State streets.

By 1844, the county had expanded into a larger courthouse, a structure constructed with local quarry stone. That courthouse was located a few blocks east of the present courthouse. In 1854, the county was still expanding rapidly and another, larger, courthouse needed to be built.

The 1854 courthouse was designed by architect John M. Van Osdel. It was a three-story, limestone building topped by an octagonal cupola. It was destroyed by fire in 1890. Fortunately, the county's records were saved, having been stored for the evening in the building's fire-resistant vaults. Many counties hastened to construct such vaults after the Great Chicago Fire of 1871 when Cook County lost thousands of irreplaceable official records.

Above Left: Harrington's Tavern served as the county's temporary courthouse. The post office also was housed in the building.

Above Right: The 1854 courthouse was the county's first instance of hiring a professional architect to direct the design and construction of the building. (Library of Congress, American Memory, Panoramic Maps Section - map of Geneva, Illinois 1869, drawn by A. Ruger.)

After the Kane County fire, the county rented a house to serve as a temporary courthouse. For several years, offices were squeezed into bedrooms, hallways, closets, and the dwelling's other nooks and crannies. Circuit court was held in the dining room.

In 1892, the Courthouse Building Committee traveled from county to county throughout Ohio, Indiana, and Michigan looking at various architects' works until they selected a Chicago architectural firm whose creations they admired. The courthouse designed by W. J. Edbrooke and Franklin P. Burnham is an impressive four-story structure made with red sandstone and brick, with terra cotta trim. A massive, 110-foot tall, rectangular dome made the courthouse the tallest building in Geneva.

In 1972, lack of space at the courthouse forced the county to buy houses in the downtown area and convert them into temporary offices. In 1975, the county's administrative staff moved their offices to a new government center. Over the past several decades, the number of county facilities has grown and several satellite government office buildings are located in and around the county seat.

In 1989 the county purchased land for a new judicial center that was designed by the architectural firm of Wight and Company. Construction on that building was completed in September 1993.

Kankakee County

Organized: February 11, 1853

County Seat: Kankakee

Named for: The Kankakee River

Left: The plan for building the present courthouse was introduced in 1907 and approved by voters in 1908. It was built on the site of the 1873 courthouse.

Inset Above: "Sherb" Noble was only thirty years old when he put up a sign that said, "All you can eat for 10 cents." His semi-frozen treat was an instant success with consumers and the first Dairy Queen franchise opened in Joliet in 1940.

Below: The outer walls of the 1855 courthouse remained standing after that building was destroyed in a fire. The walls were salvaged and reused to help build the 1873 courthouse.

Settlers moved into the Kankakee River Valley after the federal government signed the 1832 cession treaty with the Native Americans. The treaty was the final link in a long chain of treaties designed to move the Kickapoo, Pottawatomi, Winnebago, and Sac tribes to the west and away from white pioneers. The 1832 treaty ceremony at St. Louis signaled the militia's victory over Chief Black Hawk's ragtag band of starving warriors, who for several years had terrorized settlers in a vain attempt to reclaim hegemony over the hunting grounds of northern Illinois.

Despite the elimination of the threat of Indian attack, the county wasn't officially established until 1853. That is when the Illinois Central Railroad laid a route through the region and began running the "iron horse" on a regular basis through the territory. The arrival of the railroad was such a vital part of the county's maturation that the county seat's original name was Kankakee Depot. The name was shortened to Kankakee in 1855.

The first courthouse was completed in September 1855. That building was destroyed by fire in 1872. It was rebuilt in 1873 but razed in 1909 to make way for a new building the voters had approved the year before. The new courthouse was designed by architect Zachary T. Davis and was occupied on July 2, 1912.

Soft-serve ice cream in a cone was first introduced to the world on August 3, 1938, a hot summer day during the peak of the Great Depression. "Sherb's" ice cream parlor in downtown Kankakee displayed a sign telling customers they could have all the ice cream they could eat for 10¢ (about $1.50 in 2007). People lined up around the block. Sherwood "Sherb" Noble and his partner J. F. McCullough topped each semi-frozen ice cream treat with a little pigtail-like swirl. A new franchise business was created that day: "Dairy Queen."

Kendall County

Organized: February 19, 1841

County Seat: Yorkville

Named for: Amos Kendall, U.S. Postmaster General

Above: When expansion work is completed, the 1998 courthouse is projected to have sufficient office and court space until 2015. Kendall County is one of the fastest growing counties in the nation.

Inset Above: The Kendall County Administrative Building is located on the square nearby the old 1864 courthouse building.

Yorkville, a centrally-located town, was picked as the first county seat. The county leased a house from Daniel Johnson and converted it into a courthouse. The commissioners agreed to use $30 (about $750 in 2007) of the county's money to purchase benches and other improvements to make the building suitable for county business.

In 1845, several other communities stepped forward to challenge Yorkville's right to remain as the county seat. A run-off election was held to decide the issue but voting irregularities, including excessive stuffing of the ballot boxes, disqualified the results. A second election had to be held.

The town of Oswego won the right to be the new county seat. This was perhaps strange because Oswego is located near the northern border of the county and surely would soon prove to be an unpopular location for those living in the southern part of the county who had business at the county seat. Nevertheless, the election results were certified and a courthouse was constructed there in 1847.

By 1859, many citizens indeed had grown disenchanted with the location of the county seat. A new election was held and the voters returned the county seat to its old Yorkville location.

Architect O. S. Finnie was hired to design a new courthouse at Yorkville. That building was completed in 1864, during the waning days of the Civil War. It was destroyed by fire in 1887. Architect Henry Hebard designed a replacement courthouse that incorporated the still-standing walls of the burned-out building.

In 1954, two wings were added to the building to provide additional room but it soon was clear that even more space would be needed. In 1975, a separate three-story office building was constructed nearby and some county administrative offices were transferred to that structure.

Court functions were moved to a new courthouse in 1998. The architect for the project was Healy, Snyder & Bender. In 2008, work on expanding the center was in progress. Kluber Skahan & Associates provided the plans for the expansion. The historic 1864 courthouse building continues to house several offices for regional, state, and federal organizations that provide services to county residents.

The historic 1864 courthouse is home for the Kendall County Forest Preserve, Kendall and Grundy Regional Office of Education, and the Veteran's Affairs Commission.

An Illustrated History

Left: The 1884 courthouse at Galesburg stands on land purchased from Knox College. The college was the site of the fifth debate between Abraham Lincoln and Stephen A. Douglas in 1858.

Inset Left: In 1904, a memorial to Mary Ann Bickerdyke was placed on the courthouse lawn. A Knox County native, Bickerdyke volunteered as a nurse during the Civil War. She tirelessly tended the wounded, set up field hospitals, and raised funds for better medical treatment. When General Phillip Sherman's staff complained about her indifference to army regulations, he said, "She outranks me. I can't do a thing in the world."

Knox County

Organized: January 13, 1825

County Seat: Galesburg

Named for: Henry Knox, U.S. Secretary of War

Below: The Knoxville courthouse, right, was built in 1840. The Hall of Records building was added in 1854. After the county seat was shifted, the courthouse was used as an opera house for a time. (Historic American Buildings Survey: 1936 copy of 1870 photograph. Library of Congress)

In 1832, the county seat was located at Henderson, a town only a few miles southeast of Galesburg. The town's name was changed to Knoxville a few years later. The county built a hewn-log courthouse there, but the increased number of judicial and administrative duties soon out grew the small building. In 1836, the county clerk ran an advertisement inviting draftsmen to submit plans for a new courthouse. John Mandeville, a newcomer to the region and only twenty-two years old, won the competition. His temple-front, neoclassical building was completed in 1840.

During the 1850s, the Chicago, Burlington and Quincy Railroad ran a line through Galesburg instead of Knoxville, the county seat. Some claimed this snub of the county seat occurred because of a bribe. True or not, Galesburg benefited as commerce and trade that Knoxville had previously enjoyed began to migrate to the new train depot and away from the county seat.

In 1869, the question of relocating the county seat was placed before the voters. Excessive ballot stuffing at both Galesburg and Knoxville muddied the results. Law suits were filed and the issue began its slow trek through the courts. In 1873, the Illinois Supreme Court declared Galesburg the victor.

The county's records were moved to Galesburg and the city purchased land from Knox College as a site for a new courthouse. E. E. Meyers was the architect. Work began in 1884 and the new courthouse was dedicated in the early months of 1887.

Above Left: In 1895, a telephone was installed in the 1878 courthouse. The state-of-the-art handset served the entire building. (Photograph: Library of Congress, HABS section)

Above Right: Lake County's main government complex buildings include the Babcox Justice Center, the court annex, and administrative offices.

Below: The 1844 temple-front courthouse was reserved for court functions. The next door office and storage building was added in 1853. (Photograph: Library of Congress, HABS section)

Lake County

Organized: March 1, 1839

County Seat: Waukegan

Named for: The many lakes in the area

In April 1840, the court met for its first session in a schoolhouse at the temporary county seat at Independence Grove (now Libertyville). In 1841, the county seat was moved to the town of Little Fort (now Waukegan) and court sessions were held in rented rooms in the Kingston Building.

In 1844, the county constructed its first courthouse on land purchased from the federal government. That building was a temple-front design with a wood tower. The county auctioned land around the town square to pay the construction cost of $4,000 (about $92,700 in 2007). That building was used exclusively for court sessions, but it did include a jail.

In 1853, the county constructed an office building on a lot next door to the courthouse. That building also was used to store the county's records. In 1875, the courthouse was destroyed by a fire and the fact that the two buildings were separate surely saved the county records from destruction. After the conflagration, there was some discussion about moving the county seat to a more central location, but the question never generated enough heat to warrant presenting the issue to the people for a vote. The commissioners affirmed Waukegan's claim as the rightful county seat and moved ahead with work on a new courthouse.

H. C. Koch was selected as the architect. He incorporated some portions of the old courthouse walls in the new building and the courthouse was completed in 1878. That courthouse served the county until 1967 when it was razed to make way for the current structure. Today, the county is served by a complex that covers all of one block and part of another. Various architectural and engineering firms have been involved in designing the buildings in the extensive complex, including Daniel & Robison Architects, Sutter & Schroeder Architects, and the Sverdrup Corporation.

An Illustrated History | 83

LaSalle County

Organized: January 15, 1831

County Seat: Ottawa

Named for: Robert Cavelier, Sieur de La Salle, French Explorer

Above: The 1881 courthouse today is reserved for court functions.

Inset Above: Administrative offices and other courts are located at the new Criminal Justice Center.

84 | Illinois Courthouses

Left: The 1834 courthouse was a frame building. The previous courthouse was a hewn-log structure.

Right: The 1842 courthouse was the county's first brick courthouse. The cupola reached sixty feet above street level.

In 1831, LaSalle County's eastern border abutted the western edge of Cook County. But, as was the case with all of the larger counties, it was whittled down in size over the years as new counties were created from its bulk. At the same time that Illinois was increasing its number of counties, a speculative bubble—focused on canal and railroad construction—was firing up the expansionist appetites of legislators in Illinois and several other midwestern states. The upshot was passage of a vast Internal Improvement Act that the Illinois legislators passed in 1837. It was a ten million dollar plan that state legislators hoped would be enough to finance a north to south railroad line from Galena to Cairo and an east to west ninety-six-mile-long canal that would connect Lake Michigan with the Illinois River, enabling barge traffic from Chicago to New Orleans. The railroad portion of the plan was ill starred and had to be shelved for several years following the economic crash of 1837, but work on the canal resumed in 1840.

LaSalle County was one of the few areas that profited from the government project. Ottawa, the county seat, became a boom town as workers flocked to work on the big ditch. LaSalle, a nearby town, was the terminus of the canal and prospered as a staging area for freight and passengers traveling up and down the canal.

The first two courthouses constructed in Ottawa were log buildings. The 1834 courthouse was a two-story, 24 by 16 foot, frame building. Things got fancier in 1839 when the next courthouse was erected. That building was constructed with brick and featured a temple-front portico with columns and tower. The builder was William Flag. The budget for the building was $20,000 (about $400,000 in 2007). That initial estimate turned out to be low and the actual construction cost was about double that amount. This building was destroyed by a fire in 1881.

The present courthouse, standing on the same site as the first three, was built during the years 1881 to 1883. The architect was M. L. Beers. In recent years, a Criminal Justice Center and Administrative Offices Building have been built away from the downtown area but the old downtown courthouse continues to operate.

The 1888 courthouse's cornerstone was laid twice due to missteps in passing the bonds needed to pay for the project and subsequent changes in plans during its construction.

Lawrence County

Organized: January 16, 1821

County Seat: Lawrenceville

Named for: James Lawrence, War of 1812 naval hero

In 1821, Lawrence County's first court was held at the home of Toussaint Dubois, the county clerk. Certainly it was not to comment on Dubois's hospitality, but when the court convened its next session two months later, the first item on the agenda was to order the construction of a courthouse.

The court hired H. M. Gillian to build the structure, but Gillian decided to surrender the contract in December 1823 to Onates Chafie and Joshua Eaton. The two men performed the work under the same arrangement that Gillian had agreed to and the courthouse was accepted by the court in July 1824. However, after occupying the building for only a few months, the court decided it was not built well and they abandoned it. During the next two years, the court met at various homes around the community. In 1826, the court hired Joshua Bond to renovate the abandoned building and make it suitable for use again as a courthouse.

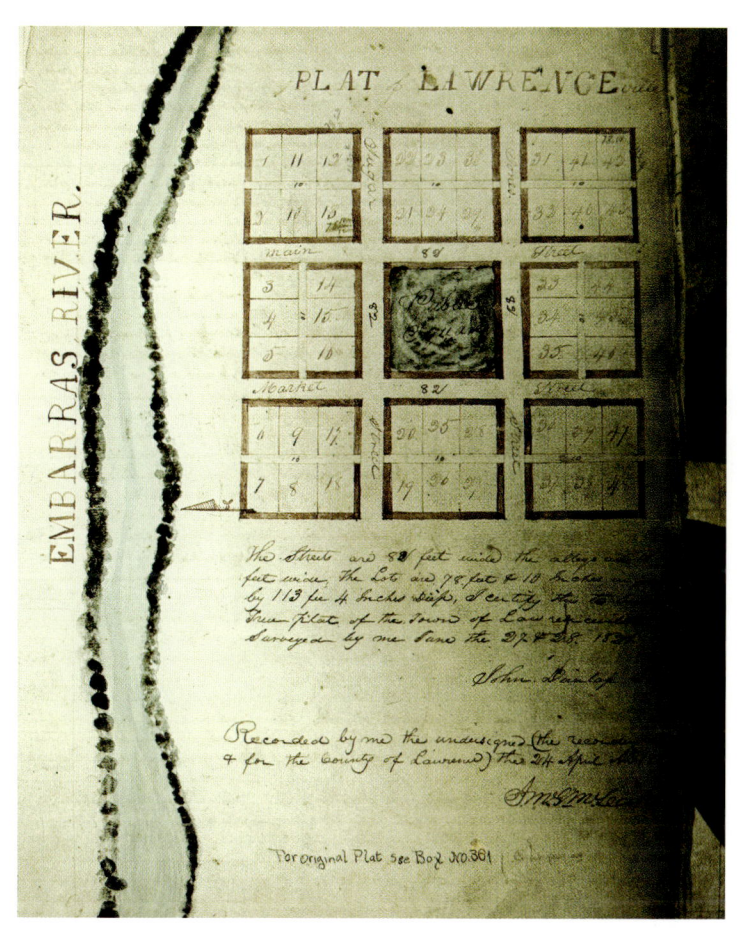

The 1821 plat of the county seat is stored in the courthouse. The numbered lots are indicated in the square "blocks" that surround the town square, which is the central block colored with green ink.

In 1840, work began on a second courthouse. That building was completed in 1842 and served the county well for the next forty years.

By 1886, the court had outgrown the old courthouse and there was concern for the lack of fireproof vaults to store the court records. The court authorized remodeling of the old building to install those features. Interestingly, the members of the Courthouse Building Committee had their own ideas about how to go about it. Evidently, they interpreted the word "remodel" to mean "build a new courthouse." They hired architect J. W. Gaddis and moved full steam ahead.

Meanwhile, citizens were flabbergasted by the committee's hubris and filed a complaint with the circuit court. A court injunction was issued and the expectation was that the project would be put on hold until the legalities could be sorted.

The committee chose to ignore the court order and went ahead with issuing contracts to start work on Gaddis's plan. As a sop to the irate citizens, and by then angry judge, they did schedule an election to vote on bonds to pay for the work. Their "end around" plan failed. The bond issue plan was soundly defeated by the voters.

This might have stopped a less determined group, but, undaunted, the committee ordered Gaddis to continue with his plans even though there was no money in the pipeline to pay him. Gaddis could see the project was disintegrating rapidly and he decided to sue the county for his fee, which stalemated the project with additional legal hang-ups. After two years of wrangling, new commissioners were elected to office and the voters decided they had made their point. They passed the bond issue and shortly afterwards the building's cornerstone was dedicated.

But, as it turned out, this classic donnybrook of dysfunctional behavior was not yet ready to fold its tent. The bond issue was insufficient to cover the cost of Gaddis's design. So, the work that had been done on the courthouse was torn down and the project began anew. The cornerstone was placed a second time. The handsome courthouse that now stands on the square is a less expensive design submitted by the McDonald Brothers, a rival architectural firm.

Lee County

Organized: February 27, 1839

County Seat: Dixon

Named for: General "Light Horse" Harry Lee

Before Lee County was formally authorized by the General Assembly in 1839, the court had already started holding meetings at James Wilson's blacksmith shop in Dixon, the de facto county seat. Even though the local officials had started making decisions as if they were a separate political entity, technically they were still under the jurisdiction of the Ogle County court. It must have been a confusing time because Ogle County itself was still getting its own affairs in order after being separated from Jo Daviess County only three years earlier.

John Dixon, a land speculator, played an active hand in the formation of Lee County. The county seat was named Dixon in exchange for his donation of eighty acres. That land was auctioned to pay for the construction of a courthouse. Dixon also presented the county a choice block of land to serve as the town's center and site for the courthouse.

Work on the first courthouse began in January 1840. Samuel M. Bowman's bid was selected. When the commissioners specified that brick was to be used instead of native stone, Bowman increased his bid by $810 to a total of $7,610 (about $163,000 in 2007). About the same time, the court also ordered construction of a jail and that work was done by Zenas Applington and G. G. Holbrook. The cost of the jail was $1,500 (about $32,000 in 2007).

Court was held in a local schoolhouse while construction of the courthouse was in progress. The temple-front courthouse was remodeled and expanded several times during its fifty year lifespan, but, in March 1900, it was razed to make way for the present courthouse.

The courthouse cornerstone was set on July 17, 1900. Architect for the project was Charles E. Brush. The construction cost was $103,395 and landscaping and furniture added $20,810 to the cost of the building (about $2,715,000 in 2007).

Top Left: The need to construct a new courthouse in 1900 triggered a second effort by the town of Amboy to have itself declared as the county seat. Their energetic attempt was defeated at the ballot box and Dixon remained the county seat.

Above: Cyrus G. Miner drew the plans for the 1840 courthouse portico. He was paid $3 (about $75 in 2007). In this photograph the building was decorated with red, white, and blue banners for a fourth of July ceremony.

88 | Illinois Courthouses

Above: The Livingston County Courthouse measurements are recorded in the American Historic Buildings Survey, a program that began during the Great Depression. Thanks to this program, photographs, drawings, measurements, and histories of many architecturally important structures and buildings have been preserved at the Library of Congress in Washington.

Inset Above: The county seat was named in honor of Chief Pontiac because of his resistance in 1763 to the British take over of Ottawa tribal lands around the Great Lakes at the conclusion of the French and Indian War.

Livingston County

Organized: February 27, 1837

County Seat: Pontiac

Named for: Edward Livingston, U.S. Secretary of State

On December 3, 1839, Livingston County signed an agreement with the owners of the town of Pontiac. The deal was that they would build a courthouse in exchange for their town being named as the county seat. Strange as it sounds today, it was common at the time for an individual or a group of investors to own a town. After surveying and platting a new community, speculators made good return on their investments as settlers and tradesmen purchased the subdivided property to transform it from virgin prairie into a busy town. If the town could be named as the county seat, it was almost guaranteed success because of the professional and trade businesses that the county government would attract to the community.

Timber for the first courthouse was cut at a sawmill located on the nearby Vermilion River. The river flowed through the blades of a spillway turbine or "water wheel." The force of the running water supplied power to the saw blade. A continuous leather belt connected the turbine to the big circular blade as it ripped the seasoned lumber into beams, trusses, and planks. The finished two-story building was 22 by 30 feet in diameter. It was accepted by the county on July 23, 1842.

Whenever court was not in session, the commissioners allowed the building to be used for town meetings and social gatherings. In 1845, the multi-use policy may have gotten a tad out of hand when Hugh Taylor put a store in the courthouse. His rent generated $3 (about $85 in 2007) per month for the county but evidently the commissioners received complaints about allowing a commercial business to operate in the courthouse. Taylor's lease was not renewed.

In 1875, construction began on the current courthouse. The building is included in the 1930s Historic American Buildings Survey. The Library of Congress record reads: "the building is in the Second Empire style with pavilions capped by mansard roofs. The foundation and upper walls are brick with limestone trim used in the water table, string courses, quoins and door and window arches. The spandrels of the corner pavilions are parged (plastered or whitewashed) in stucco."

The architect was John C. Cochrane, a noted regional architect who also helped design the 1868 Illinois Statehouse and the 1870 Iowa State Capitol.

The Civil War Monument was erected on the courthouse lawn in 1902. Street widening over the years has left it stranded on a triangular concrete island in the roadway.

Logan County

Organized: February 15, 1839

County Seat: Lincoln

Named for: John Logan, father of General John A. Logan

Postville was founded in 1835, four years before the county was formally organized. It was a well-situated town, near the geographic center of the county, and the odds on favorite to be named as the county seat in an upcoming vote in the General Assembly. The town's proprietor, Sam Tinsley, sweetened the deal by offering to build a courthouse at his expense. Even with this incentive, it was a close call. Postville was selected by a margin of one vote in the assembly.

In 1840, Tinsley built a wood frame, two-story courthouse as promised. Actually, his courthouse was in operation even before the town was legitimately named as the county seat. The legislators did not get around to formally passing the enabling legislation until several years after their floor vote. The General Assembly was busy moving the state capital from Vandalia to Springfield that year and some paperwork probably was postponed until after the move.

In 1848, Mount Pulaski, a town eleven miles southeast of Postville, challenged to be named as the new county seat. Mount Pulaski won the election.

The county sold the old Postville courthouse and it was used as a residence for many years. The historic building, scene of many trials involving Abraham Lincoln during his circuit riding law career, was purchased in 1929 by Henry Ford and moved to Dearborn, Michigan. It remains there today as part of Ford's Greenfield Village. During the 1950s, the State of Illinois erected a replica building at Postville.

In 1848, a Greek-Revival style courthouse was built at Mount Pulaski but, alas, in 1855, the railroad bypassed the county seat. The railroad ran through Lincoln instead and that city became the county seat. Lincoln had been chartered in 1853 and is the only town named for Abraham Lincoln before he was elected president. During the town's naming ceremony, Lincoln broke open a ripe watermelon and squeezed the juice onto the ground as an informal baptism of the new town.

The courthouse in Lincoln, along with much of the town, burned in 1857. A replacement courthouse, constructed on the same site, served until the turn of the twentieth century. In 1903, work began on the current courthouse and it was completed in 1905. The local firm of Dean and Ginzel designed the building.

The 1903 courthouse was completed in 1905 at a cost of $157,000 (about $3 million in 2007).

Most temple-front buildings have four columns; the portico on the 1848 courthouse has six.

The 1840 Postville courthouse was purchased by auto tycoon Henry Ford. He moved it to Dearborn, Michigan.

90 | Illinois Courthouses

Right: The WPA era courthouse was completed in 1940, shortly before the United States entered World War II.

Inset Above: A mosaic of a federal eagle is inlaid near the front entrance. The graphic design was typical of the government approved art style displayed in many 1930s public buildings.

The 1837 courthouse was built in the classic foursquare design.

The 1891 courthouse featured an asymmetric tower. The building housed both city and county government offices.

Macon County

Organized: January 19, 1829

County Seat: Decatur

Named for: Nathaniel Macon, North Carolina Senator

Macon County's first courthouse was built in 1829. It was a hewn-log building, 18 by 24 feet, and 20 feet high at the peak of the gable. The building doubled as the community's meeting hall.

Within a few years the county outgrew the facility and the county sold it in 1838 to Robert Allen who dismantled it and reassembled it at his nearby farm. The building's historic significance was appreciated years later and, in 1893, J. M. Clokey donated the structure to the Old Settlers Association. It was moved to a city park for display and it is now under the care of the Macon County Historical Society.

In 1837, the county contracted with Leonidas Munsell to build a new courthouse. That structure was a classic foursquare type building—forty by forty foot, two-stories high, brick, and with a cupola and bell. The courtroom was on the second floor. That courthouse served the county for more than fifty years.

The county's third courthouse was erected in 1891. The building was somewhat of a rarity in that it housed both the city and county governments. The façade was covered with gray limestone and featured an asymmetric tower.

Work on the present courthouse began in 1939. It was one of the six courthouses in Illinois constructed with assistance from the federal Works Progress Administration. The other WPA courthouses are at Bureau, Hamilton, Gallatin, Jefferson, and Massac counties. Two architectural firms—Acshauer & Waggoner and Charles Harris & Associates—supervised the Macon project.

An Illustrated History | 91

The 1868 Macoupin County Courthouse is larger than the 1853 statehouse at Springfield.

Macoupin County

Organized: January 17, 1829

County Seat: Carlinville

Named for: Native American word for local edible plant

The county's first courthouse was an 18 by 24 foot, log building. It was built in 1820 by Seth Hodges at a cost of $128.66 (about $2,800 in 2007). By 1829, when the county was chartered by the General Assembly, the old building was inadequate and a larger courthouse had to be built in 1830 (some records say 1838). The second courthouse was a foursquare style building—fifty by fifty foot, brick, and two stories tall. The Weatherford brothers, Harbird and Jefferson, were the builders.

The current courthouse, constructed between 1868 and 1870, was designed by architect Elijah Myers in 1867. The eclectic building quickly gained wide recognition as one of the nineteenth century's architectural marvels and it still attracts tourists, architects, and historians from around the world.

The vast court chamber features a massive, seven-foot tall, hand carved, walnut chair behind a marble bench. Electric lights were installed in the building in 1927.

The 1830s courthouse served the county for about thirty years.

The cost of the neoclassical building was a staggering amount for this period of time, an estimated $1,380,500 (about $19 million in 2007). Myers, a noted and well respected architect with an international reputation, earned an astronomical fee of over $50,000 (about $725,000 in 2007). He also designed the McDonough County Courthouse (1872) and drew the plans for other major public buildings such as the Michigan, Colorado, and Texas state capitols.

While it was being built, the true cost of the structure was hidden from the public. The initial $50,000 bond issue was quickly depleted by construction expenses. The dome and roof alone cost over $125,000. By the time the building was completed in 1870 its cost had climbed to over $1.34 million. At the time of its construction the Macoupin courthouse was considered to be the largest courthouse in the USA. Based on a 1991 Historic American Buildings Survey, the building has a 186 by 96 foot wide "footprint" and reaches a height of 167 feet at the top of its dome. The courthouse doors and window frames are made of iron and the building's skeletal frame is made from wrought iron. The outer walls are covered with Joliet limestone. The dome and roof are covered with sheet metal.

Once the public became aware of the actual cost, graft was alleged but it appears that most, if not all, of the money actually was spent on the grandiose structure. George H. Holiday, a heretofore trusted member of the four man building committee, left town without notice and was never heard from again. The other members of the committee faced down the outrage, swearing they were innocent of any wrong doing. The county finally paid off the debt on the building in 1910, forty years after the building had been completed.

Despite the subterfuge associated with the building's cost, there might have been an upside to the whole affair. The building is a unique example of a bygone age. And, as the Historic American Buildings Survey report notes, "Since its completion, it has required no new additions and requires little funding in the way of maintenance expense, so perhaps it was money well spent."

Life-size iron pelicans decorate stair balusters. In the nineteenth century, the pelican was considered a Christian symbol, representing the Eucharist. According to legend, in time of famine a mother pelican would draw blood from her own chest to feed her chicks.

An Illustrated History | 93

Madison County

Organized: September 14, 1812

County Seat: Edwardsville

Named for: James Madison, U.S. President

Robert G. Kirsch designed the 1913 courthouse. Leo A. Daly designed the 1990 administrative building that is now linked to the courthouse by a common entrance.

Edwardsville's origins were humble. Thomas Kirkpatrick built the first home there in 1805. In 1809, the community's namesake, Ninian Edwards, the governor of Illinois during its years as a territory, established his home there. Edwards later was elected as a U.S. Senator from Illinois and was returned again to the governor's office in 1826 after Illinois had entered the Union. One of his sons was a brother-in-law to Abraham Lincoln, being married to a sister of Mary Todd, and another of his sons founded A. G. Edwards, an investment firm with headquarters located at St. Louis.

Right: The overall design style of the courthouse exemplifies the second classical revival of the early twentieth century but this doorway decoration contains elements of French Baroque styling that can be traced to eighteenth-century buildings such as the Palace at Versailles.

In 1812, when President James Madison authorized the formation of Madison County, its boundaries stretched across two-thirds of the state. That enormous area was mostly a wilderness as far as the white man was concerned and what little law there was to be had was administered from old Tom Kirkpatrick's one room cabin in Edwardsville, the first county seat. The county's current boundaries were set in 1829.

A hewn-log jail was built in 1814 and Madison County erected its first courthouse in 1817, another timber structure.

In 1821 work began on a replacement courthouse, a two-story, brick structure. That building was nicknamed the "Donation Courthouse" because the county ran out of funds and it wasn't finished until 1835 when twenty-three local businessmen dug into their own pockets to pay for its completion. A third courthouse was built in 1857. Abe Lincoln spoke there in 1858 during his senatorial campaign against Stephen A. Douglas.

The present courthouse, a Second Renaissance Revival structure of white marble, was built in 1913. The Madison County Administrative Building that connects with the courthouse was erected in 1990.

An Illustrated History | 95

Marion County

Organized: January 24, 1823

County Seat: Salem

Named for: Francis Marion, the "Swamp Fox" of the American Revolution

Above: Several executions have been held on the courthouse lawn. A county official says that when he works late at the courthouse he hears footsteps in the empty hallways.

Inset Above: The cannon guarding the lobby of the courthouse is a relic from the 1862 Battle at Shiloh.

Aaron Hick built Marion County's first courthouse in 1824. It was a one and one-half story, 20 by 30 foot, hewn-log structure. The half-story upper floor was a place to hold prisoners awaiting trial. The building did not have any windows and the door was left open for ventilation. This allowed air to circulate but it also allowed the free-ranging hogs and geese of the village to make themselves at home in the building when court was not in session. Chasing away the livestock became part of a lawyer's day in court.

In 1837, the county built its second courthouse. This was a two-story, square, wood frame building. Mark Tully, one of the commissioners, was supposed to be the contractor but he surrendered his interest in the contract to Nathaniel Adams who built the courthouse.

Top: The 1824 courthouse was built without windows.

Middle: The square-sided 1837 courthouse was razed to make way for the 1858 building.

Bottom: The 1858 courthouse design combined elements of several neo-classical styles.

Construction on the third courthouse also involved a change in contractors. In 1858, J. A. Miller began work on the $35,000 building (about $695,000 in 2007) but county officials sacked him because he allegedly was using inferior materials to inflate his profit. The contracting firm of Moore and Morrow finished the job.

The cornerstone for the present courthouse was set on October 29, 1910. Joseph W. Royer was the architect. The building was renovated in 1978 with the guidance of the architectural firm of Field, Goldman and Magee. That firm also designed the 11,644 square foot, two-story, county office building that was built that same year.

Marshall County

Organized: January 19, 1839

County Seat: Lacon

Named for: John Marshall, Chief Justice of the Supreme Court

Left: The courthouse as it looks today. It began life as a rectangular building with a portico and columns.

Inset Above: The Marshall County Courthouse was remodeled in 1881 to its present transept configuration. The tower structure was removed sometime in the twentieth century.

Below: Sheriff Rob Russell stands at the base of the twin iron stairs that were installed during the 1881 renovation.

Marshall County was organized on the sly. The men behind the move realized that when the new county was created it would involve peeling land from neighboring Putnam and Tazewell counties. It was no secret that the executives in those counties would not take kindly to having even a few of their taxpayers subtracted from their tax lists. The deed had to be done before those counties had time to mount a protest or gerrymander their boundaries around their richest farmland.

In addition to losing tax revenue, county officials resisted having their boundaries redrawn because a change in the geographic center of the county opened the door for contests over relocating the county seat. Best if sleeping dogs were left undisturbed.

Knowing all of this, the "Lacon committee," began their stealthy move by handpicking and electing a sympathetic legislator to the General Assembly. Once their man was in office, he quickly filed a bill for establishing Marshall County. The enabling bill was introduced before the legislature in December 1838 and signed into law on January 19, 1839. Putnam and Tazewell residents discovered they had given birth to a new county before most of them knew they were "expecting."

The new county's first courthouse was completed on December 8, 1840. The firm of White and Shepherd built the 40 by 55 foot structure. In 1847, that building was destroyed by a fire caused by sparks from a defective chimney flue. Work on a new courthouse began immediately and a new temple-front style courthouse was completed in 1853. That building, renovated and expanded in 1881, provides the core structure for the present courthouse.

Mason County

Organized: January 20, 1841

County Seat: Havana

Named for: George Mason, father of the Bill of Rights

Above Left: During the 1950s the courthouse was a stand alone building, painted white. (Library of Congress, HABS section)

Above Right: The courthouse and storage building were joined into one structure in 1962.

Below: The 1851 courthouse was destroyed by fire in 1882. A record storage building was constructed to the right of the courthouse in 1887. The lawn also contained an auctioneer stand where cattle and reprocessed property could be sold. (Karl Collection)

A small island, similar in shape to a map outline of the island of Cuba, sat in the middle of the Spoon River near where that stream joined the Illinois River. Settlers called the little island "Cuba" and when a town sprang up nearby it was promptly dubbed "Havana."

In 1841, Havana was selected as Mason County's first county seat. It was a close race and the outcome displeased the people of Bath, a downstream town that also desired to be named as the county seat. Two years later, the outcome of the close election was still being hotly debated. To settle the matter, the county held a second election and Bath was victorious. According to an 1879 history of Mason County, the people of Bath erected a "substantial brick courthouse," but no illustration of that building is available. In due time the county's records were transferred from Havana to Bath and the county's business was conducted in that town for several years.

Havana's residents meanwhile continued to fume about the outcome of the second election and, this time, it was they who cried loudly for a "do-over." For the next several sessions of the Illinois General Assembly, Havana citizens petitioned for a new election. The General Assembly finally acquiesced and authorized the question to be on the next ballot. Fearing the outcome of the upcoming election, the Bath contingent tried to stack the deck by inserting the name of an imaginary town on the ballot to split the vote, but, in 1851, Havana's larger voting population carried the day. They reclaimed the county seat.

The first courthouse in Havana was a frame structure that was built by Walter Dray in 1851. That building was destroyed by fire in 1882 and replaced by a similar structure that same year.

In 1887, the county built a record storage building a few feet from the courthouse. In 1962, the two buildings were joined and the exterior of the combined building was given a new brick exterior.

Massac County

Organized: February 8, 1843

County Seat: Metropolis

Named for: Fort Massac, colonial military outpost on the Ohio River

Fort Massac originally was built by the French during their colonial period in North America. It was situated on a strategic spot on the Ohio River, only forty miles from where that stream flowed into the Mississippi River. The fort passed into the hands of the British as a prize of the French and Indian War. It fell into American hands after the War of Independence.

In 1843, the county board was holding its meetings at a private home in Metropolis. The circuit court heard cases at the Methodist Church. The county needed a courthouse.

Above: The 1942 courthouse was one of the last of the WPA projects in Illinois. The federal program was discontinued in 1943.

Inset Above: Now a famous Metropolis landmark, the Superman statue is located on the courthouse square.

100 | Illinois Courthouses

Right: In 1757, the French raised Fort De L'Ascension during the French and Indian War. The British built Fort Massac atop the ruins of the French fort. In 1778, the outpost fell into American hands when George Rogers Clark secured the territory for the United States during the Revolutionary War. The old fort's site became Illinois' first state park.

Below: The 1862 courthouse was a handsome building that served the community for nearly eighty years. In later years the spire was removed. (Massac County Historical Society)

Samuel Arnont submitted a design in June 1843 and construction began early in July. The record is vague as to the appearance of that courthouse but the specifications for a jail built that same year called for it to be constructed with good hewn timber, one foot thick, and with dove-tailed corners. It is likely that the buildings were similar in material and construction style.

Massac County constructed a second courthouse in 1862 and it served the community until March of 1940. It was razed to make way for the present courthouse. That building, funded by a Works Progress Administration grant, was occupied on July 29, 1942.

The word "metropolis" is a Greek word that means "mother city." Metropolis, the county seat of Massac County, may not qualify for that title, but it can boast of something that sets it apart from all other cities. Its favorite son is Superman!

In 1972 the city received permission from National Periodical Publications to use its copyrighted Superman image and logo to promote both the city and Superman. Before the program could "up, up and away," the 1973 oil embargo delivered a dose of economic Kryptonite. The plan for a $50 million Superman theme park was tabled and Superman's famous red cape was put into mothballs.

Refusing to surrender their super dream, in 1993 the community erected a 15 foot tall bronze statue of Superman next to the county courthouse. This statue has become ground zero for Metropolis's annual Superman celebration.

An Illustrated History | 101

McDonough County

Organized: January 25, 1826

County Seat: Macomb

Named for: Commodore Thomas McDonough

A ramshackle alehouse operated by a Baptist preacher served as the first meeting place for the county court at Washington (later renamed Macomb). The Reverend James Baker's establishment was a rough hut barely able to keep the rain out and, as quickly as possible, the county ordered construction of a courthouse. In 1830, Sheriff William Southward built the structure for a fee of $69.50 (about $1600 in 2007). The 18 by 20 foot, hewn-log building was not a great improvement over Baker's tavern but the roof did not leak and the court's audience was mostly sober.

In 1834, the court issued a contract to Joseph Updegraff for the construction of a foursquare courthouse. He built a two-story, 46 by 46 foot, square building with a cupola. Updegraff's courthouse was of brick construction and the masonry work took several seasons to complete. Cement did not cure well during the cold and rainy months of the year and laying the courses of brick was usually done only when the weather was likely to be reasonably dry for an extended period of time.

The courthouse was available for community meetings. The sheriff was in charge of deciding who would be allowed to use the building but he was instructed to deny entrance to lewd and tasteless activities such as "shows, slight of hand, or theater performances."

By 1868, after thirty-two years of service, the old courthouse was worn out and needed to be replaced. How to pay for a new building stirred up a debate. The residents in the county throught the residents of the town should pay more and a clash of wills ensued. The verbal dust-up between the mayor of Macomb and the county commissioners encouraged the town of Bushnell to mount a drive to be named as the new county seat, but they were unsuccessful in securing enough votes. The contest refocused the town and county executives and the financial issues were soon settled.

Construction of a new courthouse proceeded and was completed in 1872. Elijah Myers, the man who designed the "million dollar" courthouse for Macoupin County, was the architect. His original design included a handsome mansard roof, but after being damaged in a storm in 1890, the structure was refitted with a pitched roof.

Above: In 1973, the courthouse was restored to its original red brick and white stone trim appearance.

Inset Above: A mansard roof capped the building originally, but it was changed after being damaged by a storm in 1890.

Below: The fence around the 1834 courthouse yard kept horses and livestock from munching the grass.

McHenry County

Organized: January 16, 1836

County Seat: Woodstock

Named for: William McHenry, soldier and politician

Above: The current courthouse and seat of justice for McHenry County.

Inset Above: In 1895, Eugene V. Debs spent six months in the Woodstock jail. Debs, a union organizer, read Karl Marx while in prison and became one of the best-known socialists in the United States. He ran for president five times. (Library of Congress, Prints and Photographs Division)

Below: The decommissioned 1857 courthouse anchors Woodstock's historic downtown cultural district.

After the War of 1812, white settlers entered Illinois in greater numbers. The state's total population more than tripled to 150,000 between 1820 and 1830. The rich prairie land and mining districts of northern Illinois were particularly attractive. The U.S. government signed a series of cession treaties with Native American tribes trying to head off trouble with the Indians as settlers advanced into tribal hunting grounds. After Black Hawk and his band were defeated in 1832, the hegemony of Native American tribes in Illinois ended and northern counties such as McHenry received a steady influx of new settlers.

McHenry County's original boundaries stretched east to the shore of Lake Michigan and west to the area that became Boone County. The county's present boundaries were set in 1839. The first seat of justice was at the town of McHenry and a frame courthouse was built there.

In 1844, that building was hoisted off its foundation and hauled to Centerville (later renamed Woodstock). The county seat had to be relocated when Lake County was formed in 1839, reducing McHenry County's size by half. Woodstock became the more centrally-located town and was given the title of county seat.

The repositioned Centerville courthouse countinued in use for a few years but, in 1857, the county built a new courthouse at Woodstock. The Italianate style building was said to resemble the 1853 Cook County Courthouse at Chicago. The courthouse's architect, John Mills Van Osdel, also designed many of Chicago's classic buildings, several of which unfortunately were destroyed in the Great Fire of 1871. Wings were added to the Woodstock courthouse in the early 1900s.

An adjoining structure, the sheriff's house and jail, was built in 1887. The jail is considered historically significant because Eugene Debs, the fiery union leader, served a six month sentence there after being convicted of violating a restraining order issued during the infamous 1895 Pullman strike. The old courthouse and jail are maintained as historic sites at the city's center.

A new McHenry County Courthouse and public safety facility was erected in 1972. The architectural firm of Johnson, Kile, Seehausen and Associates designed the building. It was expanded in 1990 under the guidance of Legat Architects and HOK.

An Illustrated History | 103

McLean County

Organized: December 25, 1830

County Seat: Bloomington

Named for: John McLean, U.S. Senator

Above: The 1976 McLean County Law and Justice Center is located a block south of the old courthouse square.

Inset Left: The 1901 courthouse stands on the old town square. The building has been preserved and now houses a museum.

Below: The rotunda dome in the old courthouse is over 100 feet high and features an allegorical painting representing peace and prosperity. An exposed stairway provides access to the dome.

The first court sessions met at the home of James Allan, the temporary seat of justice for the county seat of Blooming Grove (later renamed Bloomington). In 1832, the county court moved out of Allan's parlor and constructed an 18 by 30 foot, single-story, frame courthouse.

In 1836, the county built a brick, two-story, foursquare courthouse. Its cupola was perched atop an elevated square base and that courthouse served the county well for the next thirty years.

In 1868, the county officials decided to construct a more extravagant courthouse on the square. They hired John C. Cochrane and Alfred H. Piquenard, two well-respected and in-demand architects. While working on the McLean commission, the architects also were commissioned to design a new statehouse at Springfield. The duo later designed Iowa's 1870 statehouse. Unfortunately, the McLean County Courthouse that they created was destroyed by fire in 1900.

In 1901, ground was broken for the new courthouse as quickly as debris from the burned out building could be cleared from the site. Architects for the project were Reeves and Baillie. Their building still stands on the old courthouse square. When the present courthouse facility was built, the county donated the monumental old courthouse to the McLean County Museum of History.

The current McLean County Courthouse was designed by the firm of Lundeen, Hilfinger and Asbury and construction began in 1976. Additions in 1988 were designed by Hilfinger, Asbury, Abels and Associates and more additions were made in 1996 under the direction of Shive & Hattery, Inc.

Menard County

Organized: February 15, 1839

County Seat: Petersburg

Named for: Pierre Menard, Lieutenant Governor

Above: The present Menard County Courthouse was built in 1898.

Inset Above: Foot-thick timber beams support the courthouse roof and dome. Contractors had to have good knowledge of the load bearing capabilities of different types of wood.

Menard County was formed in 1839, the year that the first game of baseball was played in the United States. Several of the towns in Menard County competed to be named as the county seat. Two of the contenders, Huron and Miller's Ferry, were eliminated after it was determined they were actually in the newly formed neighboring county of Mason which had been created only twenty-two months after Menard County was established.

Petersburg, the eventual winner of the county seat honor, had been platted in 1836 by Abraham Lincoln. Before he took up law as a career, Lincoln had worked at a number of jobs: rail-splitter, postmaster, store clerk, militia captain, and elected state representative. He also worked part-time as a surveyor. In 1833, after his brief tour of duty in the Black Hawk War, the Sangamon County surveyor hired him as an assistant. Lincoln taught himself the math needed to be a surveyor and he preformed surveying jobs off and on until he received his law license in 1837.

Lincoln had a good reputation as an accurate surveyor. But, he did fudge at least once while working as a surveyor. While platting Petersburg, Menard County's future county seat, he drew a crooked line. He saw that a true line would result in a street right-of-way running through the middle of Jemima Elmore's house. Lincoln dog-legged the plat line to go around her home.

The county's first courthouse, as described in a history of the town, looked like "a square brick structure that was shaped like one of those old tobacco barns." That building was razed in 1896 and the present courthouse was erected in 1898.

Lincoln worked for a few years as a surveyor before taking up the practice of law. He platted Petersburg in 1836. (Artist: Lloyd Ostendorf)

An Illustrated History | 105

Lincoln, the Courthouse Lawyer

Abraham Lincoln began studying the law at the tender age of twenty-five. He may have been young by modern standards but already he had served as a captain in the 1832-1833 Black Hawk War and been elected (at twenty-three) as a state representative to the Illinois General Assembly. Living in New Salem at the time, he was still searching for a stable career. When the legislature was not in session, he clerked in a store at New Salem and worked as a surveyor to keep body and soul together.

His first brush with the law as a profession came in 1834 when a fellow legislator urged him to seriously consider becoming a lawyer. John Todd Stuart, a Springfield attorney, loaned Lincoln a few of his law books and young Mr. Lincoln diligently began to study the intricacies of jurisprudence as practiced in the Illinois court system.

In 1836, Lincoln received a license to practice law in Illinois. He took to it like a duck to water, worked hard, won the respect of his clients and other lawyers, and charged a fair price. Within a few years he was the head of one of the most successful law firms in Illinois. By the time he won the presidency in 1860, he had become one of the most successful and highest paid attorneys in the United States.

All of that took a few years however. In 1837, Lincoln left New Salem and moved to Springfield. He became a junior law partner in Stuart's office. Lincoln and Stuart's friendship had begun when they served together in the Black Hawk War and in the legislature. Stuart also was a cousin to Mary Todd, Lincoln's wife to be. Their friendship was long lasting but their partnership spanned only a few years. In 1838, Stuart won election to the first of several terms in the U.S. House of Representatives. His travels to Washington, D.C., and political interests consumed most of his time. This left Lincoln to complete his legal education on a hit and miss basis but, while under Stuart's tutelage, Lincoln fielded a garden variety of criminal and common law disputes. Stuart also introduced Lincoln to the life of a circuit riding lawyer. Together, they rode the first judicial circuit before Sangamon County was absorbed into the eighth circuit in 1839. This was the same year that Springfield became the new state capital, replacing Vandalia. Lincoln was one of the "Long Nine" legislators behind the move. It was also the year that Lincoln met Stuart's cousin, Mary Todd.

In 1841, after Lincoln and Stuart ended their partnership, Lincoln joined the office of Stephen Logan. Springfield was now the state capital and that opened the way for Lincoln to begin practicing in new areas of the law, including bringing appellant cases to the Illinois Supreme

Above: Recently commissioned statues of Lincoln reflect a more personable, relaxed image of the man. Lincoln sitting on a bench in front of the old McLean County Courthouse at Bloomington is one example. (Sculptor: Rick Harney, 2000)

Inset: Lincoln's smiling expression (detail of "Lincoln leaning on fence" statue) greets visitors to the Livingston County Courthouse. (Sculptor: Rick Harney, 2006)

Lincoln, along with other lawyers and judges, rode horses and small wagons as they traveled the route of the old eighth circuit. Court was held for a week or two. The members of the troupe usually stayed with friends for the duration and then decamped for the move to the next county. It was a vagabond life that appealed to Lincoln. Each year he left his home in Springfield to spend three months in the spring and another three in the fall traveling the circuit.

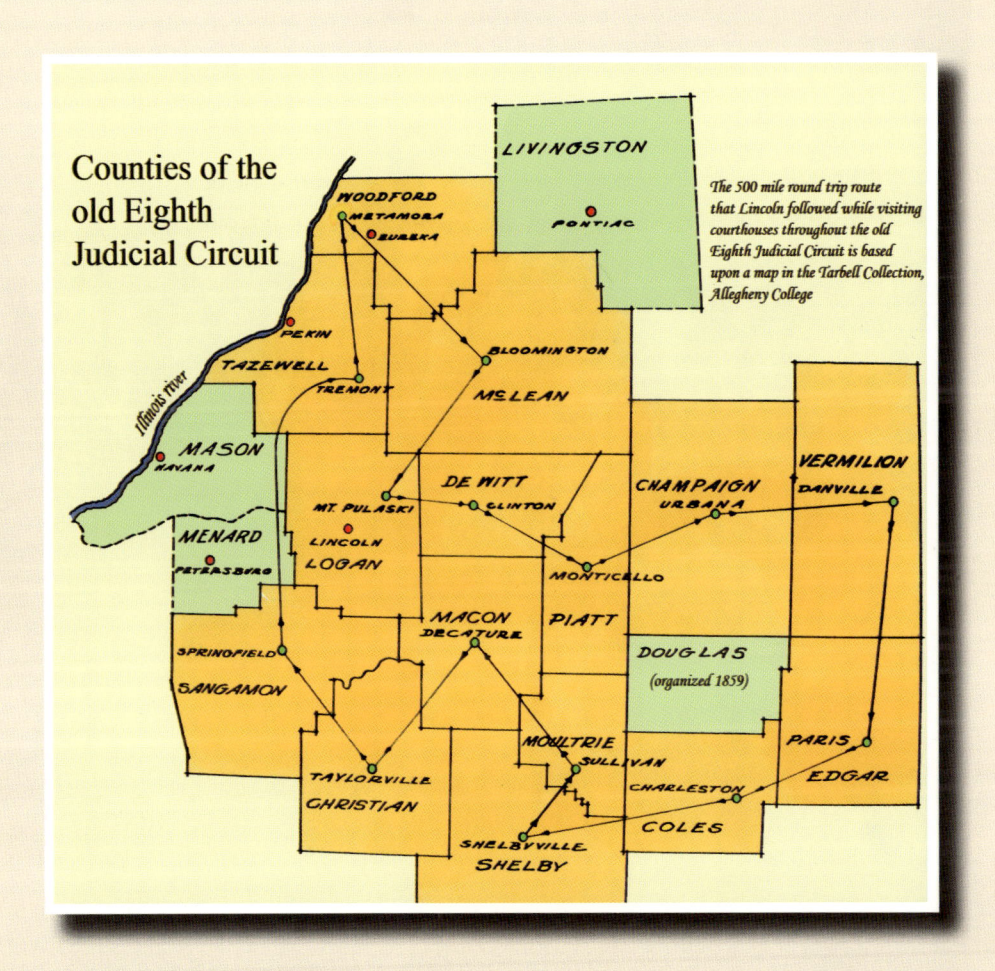

Counties of the old Eighth Judicial Circuit

The 500 mile round trip route that Lincoln followed while visiting courthouses throughout the old Eighth Judicial Circuit is based upon a map in the Tarbell Collection, Allegheny College

Court and representing clients before the federal court. During his time in Logan's office, Lincoln continued to ride the eighth circuit, traveling by horseback from one county courthouse to the next, taking cases as they came. Again the affiliation between the two lawyers lasted for only a few years. In December 1844, the men amiably dissolved their partnership so that Logan could go into practice with his son. Lincoln, who had married Mary Todd several years earlier, was of a mind to set up his own law firm.

Lincoln recruited William H. Herndon to be the junior attorney in his firm. Lincoln had known Herndon since boyhood and the younger man looked upon him almost as an older brother. Herndon had his own practice but provided order to the office while Lincoln concentrated more on preparing arguments and working with clients. They split fees equally.

For twenty-five years, beginning as a young lawyer and until 1861 when he left for Washington to assume the presidency, Lincoln spent half of each year riding the old eighth judicial circuit. The first three-month-long term began in February and the second three month session began in September.

An Illustrated History | 107

During the years that Lincoln rode the circuit, the officers of the court—the judge, state's attorneys, and lawyers—set up shop in the respective courthouses to deal with whatever cases were pending. Depending upon the amount of business to be conducted, court in each community might last from several days to a few weeks. Itinerant lawyers, such as Lincoln, either assisted local attorneys as co-counsel or dealt directly with clients seeking representation. It was not uncommon for Lincoln to serve as co-counsel with a local lawyer on one case and then argue against that same individual on the next.

Much of Lincoln's fame as a lawyer was the result of his successes on the circuit, usually concerning Lincoln's gift for securing improbable victories. In one case, Lincoln's client was sued for slander. He'd called the plaintiff a hog thief. Rather than use the argument that no such statement had been made, Lincoln instead said, yes, his client had made the statement but that it was not slander because it was the truth! The man had in fact stolen the pigs. His client was merely telling the truth. The plaintiff's lawyer, Stephen A. Douglas, caught flat-footed by the accusation, sputtered but was unable to quickly disprove the charge. The slander charge was dismissed. But, that wasn't the end of the story.

Lincoln helped establish the Republican Party in Illinois. In 1855, he paused at Shelbyville—one of his stops along the circuit—to hold a three hour debate with Anthony Thorton, a friend and fellow lawyer. They debated the young party's position concerning slavery and other topics of the day. (Artist: Robert Root, 1918)

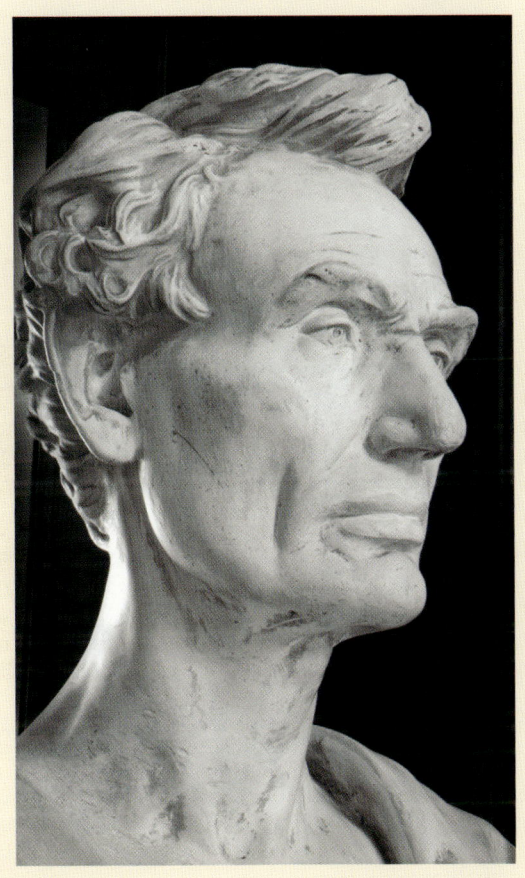

Left: One of the last images made of Lincoln before his presidency, this bust was a life copy made in 1860 and is on display at the Lee County Courthouse. Many of Illinois' courthouses have plaques, papers, portraits, and other memorabilia to commemorate a trial or speaking engagement by the martyred president. (Artist: L.W. Volk, 1860)

Right: One of Lincoln's most famous cases involved "Duff" Armstrong, a man accused of murder. Lincoln secured Armstrong's freedom by creating reasonable doubt about the veracity of a key witness's testimony. The witness swore that he had clearly viewed the murder by the light of a full moon. Lincoln produced an Old Farmer's Almanac that showed the moon was in its wane stage that night. (Artist: Lloyd Ostendorf)

Douglas's former client—now standing before the court as an accused thief—was arrested and put on trial. He could not afford to hire Douglas a second time so the court appointed an attorney to defend him. That lawyer was Mr. Lincoln, the man who had put him into jeopardy in the first place. Lincoln called a witness to collaborate his client's story about being twenty miles away when the pig thief occurred and won an acquittal for his defendant. Lincoln gained the reputation of being the only lawyer to win the same case twice, winning for both sides.

In 1857, at the height of his fame as a lawyer, Lincoln's average fee per client was $5 to $20 (about $125 to $500 in 2007). He was paid much more for his work with corporations. He earned $5,000 in one case when he was an advocate for the Illinois Central Railroad.

Lincoln suspended most of his legal work when he was busy with political matters, such as when he served a term in Congress as U.S. Representative in 1847 and again in 1858 when he took part in the famous series of debates while locked in a senatorial contest with Stephen Douglas. But, despite his time spent in various political offices before he was elected president, Lincoln always thought of himself as a lawyer rather than a professional politician.

On the day that he left for Washington to assume the presidency in 1861, he told Herndon, his devoted law partner, to continue displaying the sign that read "Lincoln and Herndon" because he wanted his old clients to know that he expected to resume his law practice when he returned; perhaps even to once again ride the eighth judicial circuit.

An Illustrated History | 109

Mercer County

Organized: January 13, 1825

County Seat: Aledo

Named for: Hugh Mercer, Revolutionary War leader

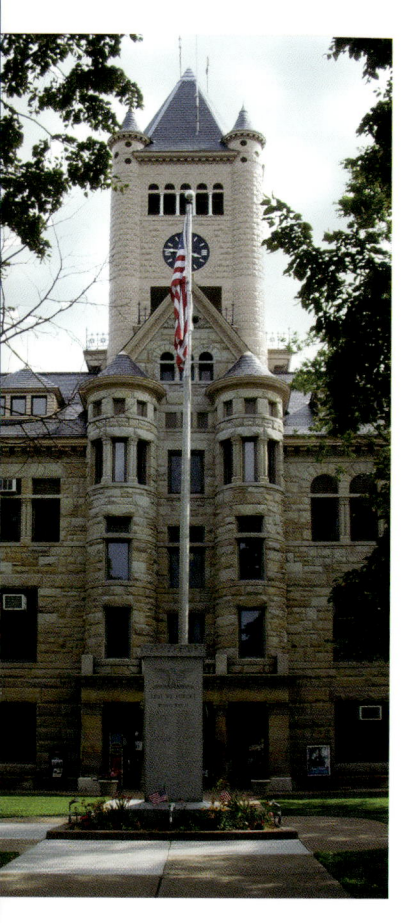

The groundwork for organizing Mercer County began while it was part of the Military Tract. The tract was a vast area of public land in central and northwestern Illinois owned by the federal government. The government parceled off 80 to 160-acre chunks as "bounty" to the veterans of the War of 1812. Settlers were hesitant to homestead there, however, until the Native Americans ceded their land to the government and left the territory. This delayed the final organization of the county until 1835. The town of New Boston was selected as a temporary county seat.

In 1837, the county seat was shifted to Millersburg, a more centrally-located community. In 1839, the county erected a two-story courthouse there.

In 1847, the location of the county seat shifted again, this time to Keithsburg. The county built a one-story, 40 by 50 foot, brick courthouse and that community served as the county seat for the next ten years.

By 1857, railroad lines were crisscrossing Illinois. New towns seemed to sprout like mushrooms almost overnight as businesses located themselves close to the train depots. The town of Aledo began as a humble depot and blossomed in such fashion.

Citizens also moved to areas close by the depot and no sooner had Aledo sprung up but it became the new seat of justice for Mercer County. Before a courthouse could be built there, the Civil War exploded across the American landscape. The residents of Mercer County decided to wait for a quieter time before constructing a new building. In the interim, a schoolhouse was drafted into service as a temporary courthouse. The interim lasted many years. In 1872, the county built a modest building to provide more office and storage space, but work on the current courthouse did not begin for another twenty-two years.

In 1894, when a new courthouse finally was built at Aledo, a statue of Lady Justice supposedly was to be placed upon a platform on the clock tower. No statue was ever placed there. This has given generations of children and wags an opportunity to ask, "Why is there no Justice in the Mercer County Courthouse?"

Above: The 1894 courthouse was designed by architect M. E. Bell. The tower and roof were refurbished in 2007.

Left: Twin turrets accent the building's main entrance. The cone shaped cap on each turret is repeated on the four corners of the clock tower.

Monroe County

Established: January 6, 1816

County Seat: Waterloo

Named for: James Monroe

Above: The Monroe County Courthouse in Waterloo.

Inset Above: The postcard sketch shows the building's profile after wings were added in 1907. (Artist: Roscoe Misselhorn)

Below: The courthouse as it appeared in 1853. (History of Randolph, Monroe and Perry Counties, Illinois, 1883)

The first public building that was built in 1818 in Monroe County was not the courthouse, but a jail. The town of Harrisonville was the temporary county seat. The jail was built by Samuel Kinkead and it was a 16 by 16 foot, hewn-log structure. He fitted iron bars in the windows and attached a double thick door that featured metal hinges that were "firmly put into the logs." Court sessions, meanwhile, were held at the home of Thomas James.

In 1825, the county decided to establish a permanent county seat at the town of Waterloo. The shift of the county seat to a new location was accompanied by a few hard feelings. One disgruntled Harrisonville official expressed his displeasure by peevishly hiding the metal lock, door hinges, and iron window bars that had been the pride of the old jail building. A decade later he sheepishly surrendered those items to the sheriff at Waterloo.

Other county officials were slow to transfer their records to the new county seat because, they said, there was no agreement yet on where to build a courthouse in Waterloo or how to pay for it. Their objections were flimsy because no courthouse had ever been built at Harrisonville either.

The hostility over the move to Waterloo was resolved eventually. The county's first courthouse was built there in 1832. It was a 30 by 36 foot, two-story, brick building. That building evidently was not well built. In 1834, the judges noticed that the walls shook when boys bounced a rubber ball against the side of the structure. The county clerk posted a proclamation forbidding children from throwing toy-balls against the courthouse walls.

Construction of the present courthouse began in 1851. Lloyd Prather was hired to do the work. His contract was unusually explicit about every detail of how the building was to be constructed. The specifications described exactly how the brick courses were to be laid, the exact number of nails to be used, how long the lumber should be cured, and how the copper sheeting on the roof was to be fastened. It appeared that the county commissioners did not want to work in another courthouse with walls that would shake if they were hit with a rubber ball. The core building has been expanded several times in the twentieth century.

An Illustrated History

The 1993 Montgomery County Courthouse houses all judicial services.

Montgomery County

Organized: February 12, 1821

County Seat: Hillsboro

Named for: Richard Montgomery, War of Independence General

One month after enabling legislation was passed to create Montgomery County, a site selection committee agreed amongst themselves that the spot on the map marked "Hamilton" was indeed the perfect spot for a county seat. The speculators who owned the property immediately hired a surveyor to plat the new town. Along with staking out property lines and right of ways, the owners built a few cabins and opened a store in anticipation of their community being named as the county seat.

However, the selection committee's choice did not please everyone who needed to be pleased. When the General Assembly reconvened, they fired the first site selection committee; rejecting their recommendation. A new site committee was appointed and soon the legislators were informed that Newton Coffey had donated twenty acres at Hillsboro. Accordingly, the county seat egg was hatched at Hillsboro and not at Hamilton.

Left: The 1868 courthouse was designed by Chicago architect G. B. Randal in "Second Empire" style.

Right: The historic courthouse continues to dominate Hillsboro's town square.

In 1823, the county paid Luke Lea Steel $344.53 1/3 (about $7,940 in 2007) to erect the first courthouse, a hewn-log structure. In 1833, the county built a replacement courthouse that featured a stone foundation and cupola. Aaron Knapp earned hard cash of $2 (about $50 in 2007) for drawing plans for the frame building and contractor Easton Whitten was paid $1,800 (about $44,000 in 2007) to build it.

In 1852, that building was remodeled. Some claimed the refit was so drastic that the building that resulted might properly be called the county's third courthouse. Brickwork replaced the wood frame and a portico with four white columns was installed at the front of the building.

The county continued to prosper and in 1868 the old courthouse was bursting at the seams. The citizenry thought the idea of a new building sounded alright but the town of Litchfield stepped forward to request that any new courthouse be built in their town instead of Hillsboro. The county commissioners sabotaged that idea by agreeing to remodel the old courthouse instead of constructing a new building. The remodeling budget was set at $9,500 (about $130,000 in 2007). The expense was to be paid by selling wetlands owned by the county. This maneuver allowed the county officials to avoid a bond election and effectively nullified Litchfield's bid, but it created an awkward pay-as-you-go funding mechanism that slowed work on the project. The building was not finished until 1872. An addition was added in 1912.

The appearance of the building has been altered over the years. The cap on the southeast tower has been removed. The upper topmost half of the left tower at the front of the building also has been removed. This building now houses only administrative offices. In 1993, a court complex was constructed a block away. That building was designed by the firm of Design Architects, Inc.

Morgan County

Organized: January 31, 1823

County Seat: Jacksonville

Named for: Daniel Morgan, War of Independence General and Politician

In 1823, a temporary county seat was established about six miles southwest of Jacksonville. The county's administrative offices and court were housed in two log cabins. The county soon shifted its offices to another temporary county seat at a town called Olmstead's Mound (later renamed Allison's Mound), but that location also proved to be unsatisfactory.

In 1825, the county officials picked Jacksonville to be the permanent county seat. At the time, the site was an open field. The first trials were held out of doors. At the conclusion of a trial, the judge sent the jury to a nearby grove of trees so they could sit in the shade and deliberate about the testimony and evidence. The pastoral accommodation had one drawback. On-lookers with an opinion to share thought they had every right to join in a jury's open air discussion and help them reach a verdict.

The first courthouse was constructed in 1826. It was a 30 by 40 foot, frame building. The building rested on a foundation made of sawed tree trunk sections that were set upright on the ground. Unfortunately, the next year a fire destroyed that building along with the county records.

In 1828, the court began the process of replacing the burned-out building. The initial plan was for a 40 by 40 foot square, brick, two-story building, but the court issued a last minute change order to increase its size to 40 by 50 feet.

All of the contractors' bids exceeded the budget, however, and the project had to be postponed until the following year. Finally, the court decided to deal with the funding hurdle by building in a piecemeal fashion. They awarded six individual contracts, which allowed for staggered payments as each section of the courthouse was completed. The finished building was accepted in September 1830.

In 1867, the county court advertised that they would pay a $100 prize (about $1,450 in 2007) for an acceptable set of plans for building a new courthouse, but that hook failed to snag an amateur with professional architectural talent. The county hired G. B. Randal, a Chicago architect.

While plans were being made for construction of a new courthouse, city leaders requested that the county turn over the old courthouse square for use as a town park. The court agreed and selected a corner lot as the site for building the new courthouse. Architect Randal adapted his plan to the new space and designed a building that would need only two entries instead of the usual four, thereby reducing the construction expense.

Formal acceptance of the building came in 1869.

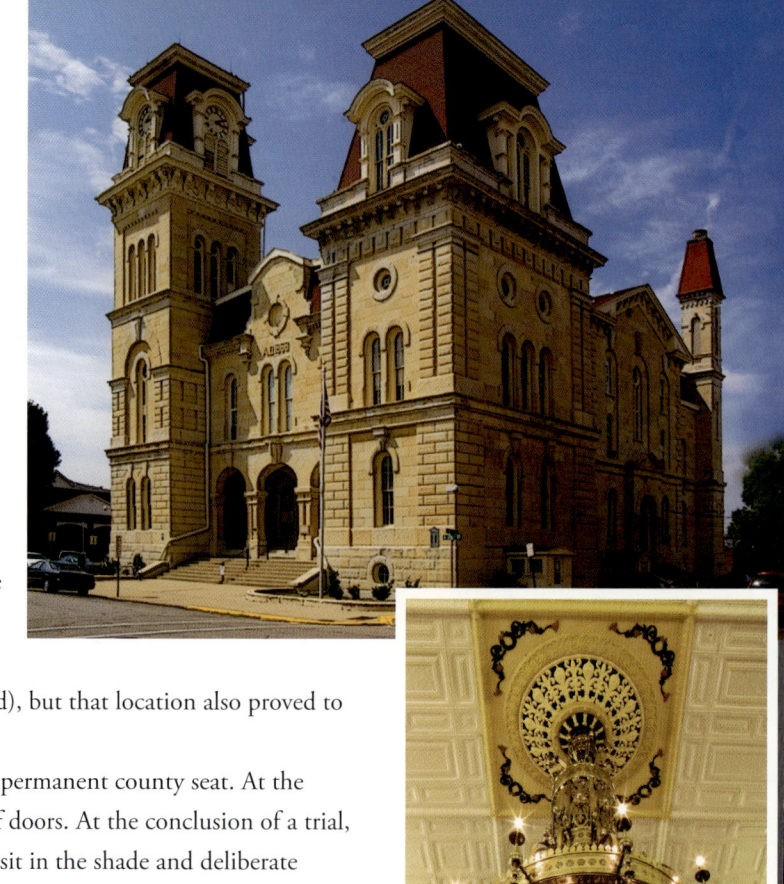

Above: G. B. Randal designed the Morgan County 1867 courthouse. He used a similar plan when he designed the 1868 Montgomery County Courthouse.

Inset Above: The chandelier in the courtroom originally was a gas-lit fixture that hung in the Centenary United Methodist Church. It was converted to electric around 1900. In 1999, the Morgan County Historical Society donated it to be used in the courtroom.

Moultrie County

Organized: February 16, 1843

County Seat: Sullivan

Named for: William Moultrie, War of Independence General

Above: During construction of the 1904 courthouse, the county's population was 15,224.

Inset Above: A mural of the 1848 courthouse decorates a wall of the second floor of the 1904 courthouse. (Moultrie County collection)

Below: An illustration of the 1865 courthouse. A one-story annex, possibly a records storage vault, was added later to the building.

Moultrie County was formed by taking land from Macon and Shelby counties. Illinois was fast approaching its present configuration of 102 counties and there were only six more yet to be created: Cumberland and Pulaski, 1843; Saline, 1847; Kankakee, 1853; and Douglas and Ford, 1859.

Moultrie County's first election of officers was held in April 1843. John Freeland, a man who seems to have had trouble saying "no," was elected to three of those offices: circuit clerk, county clerk, and recorder. Early court sessions were held at James Camfield's cabin, the temporary courthouse and county seat.

In 1844, the county seat was shifted to a town called Nelson. But, the game of musical county seats was just warming up. The next year, 1845, a new site was picked but its location was so unpopular no one seems to have made note of it and within a few months the seat of justice was moved. The next spot that was picked was a virtually uninhabited piece of land near the geographical center of the county. It was called Asa's Point, a site, ironically, that was only a few miles northeast of Camfield's cabin, the place where the court had held meetings a few years earlier. Asa's Point was renamed Sullivan and the county seat has remained at that spot.

In 1848, the county built its first courthouse in Sullivan. It was a brick, two-story, foursquare building, sans cupola. During the famous Lincoln and Douglas senatorial campaign of 1858, kismet brought the two candidates to speak at this courthouse on the same day. Neither candidate had prior knowledge of the other's plan to appear there that day. The candidates graciously managed to stay out of each other's way during the speech-giving portion of the day. That evening things were not as polite when their supporters paraded through the streets carrying torches and candidate banners. The flag-waving throngs marched directly into each other; neither side willing to give ground and let the other pass. Some signs were used as clubs and some knuckles were bloodied.

The 1848 courthouse was destroyed in a fire in 1864 and most of the county's records were lost in the blaze.

The county's second courthouse was completed in 1866. In addition to a fireproof vault, the new building was crowned with a square tower that was topped with a domed cap. The county sold some swampy ground to pay for construction of that building. That was not the lopsided deal as it might seem at first glance. The new owners quickly drained the wetlands and turned it into rich farmland.

The present courthouse was built in 1904. The Chicago firm of Dean and Ginzel served as architects for the project.

An Illustrated History | 115

Ogle County

Organized: January 16, 1836

County Seat: Oregon

Named for: Joseph Ogle, War of Independence Veteran

The town of Oregon was chosen as the county seat in 1837 but its location was not well accepted by the folks living in the southern half of the county. Rather than tolerate Oregon as their county seat, the disgruntled folks to the south petitioned the General Assembly for the right to create an entirely new county. In 1839, the legislators split Ogle County at a horseshoe bend in the Rock River and formed Lee County south of that spot. The town of Dixon became Lee County's seat of justice.

Also in 1839, for reasons unknown, the name of the county seat was changed from Oregon to Florence. In 1843, the name was switched back to Oregon. Oregon had been named in honor of the "Oregon Country," a vast northwestern region of North America that was being ruled jointly by the United States and Great Britain. Most Americans assumed that it was just a matter of time until it would become part of the United States and that officially took place by treaty between the two countries in 1846. The Northwest Mounted Police retreated to Canada.

The county erected its first courthouse in 1841. That building was put to the torch by a gang of "prairie bandits" the day before a trial was due to be held. The outlaws were one of several gangs who ranged across northern Illinois between the 1830s and the 1840s. They set the fire in an attempt to terrorize witnesses and destroy evidence that would be used against three of their members who were being held for cattle rustling.

Their plot failed. The wily court clerk had taken the evidence home with him the night before for safe keeping. The trial went forward as scheduled, but the gang's scheme was not finished.

One of the men selected for jury duty was in league with the outlaws. The bandit spy tried to subvert his fellow jurists with threats and bribes until they promised in no uncertain terms to lynch him on the spot. The three bandits were convicted and sentenced to long prison terms.

The county's second courthouse was built in 1848. It was a one-story, brick building.

The present courthouse was erected in 1891. George O. Garnsey was the architect. That building was renovated in 1984 and continues to serve the community well. A judicial center was built in 2005.

The 1891 courthouse has been renovated, but the building's original design is intact.

The 2005 Judicial Center was designed by the firm of Holabird & Root.

116 | Illinois Courthouses

Peoria County

Organized: January 13, 1825

County Seat: Peoria

Named for: The Peoria, a Native American tribe

Above: The 1962 courthouse stands on the site of the previous two courthouses.

Bottom Left: In 1850, two men were tried for murder in the 1833 courthouse and sentenced to be executed. A mob stormed the jail but one of the prisoners held them at bay—using a rock to bash the skull of anyone who tried to enter his cell. The men survived the ordeal and were hung legally a month later. (Artist: Van Norman Correll)

Bottom Right: The cornerstone for this courthouse was laid on September 30, 1876. The cost was $206,071.31 (about $4 million in 2007). (Artist: Elmer King)

In 1825, vast buffalo herds still roamed Illinois' northern prairie. Settlements were few and far between in the newly formed Peoria County and the new county seat—also named Peoria—had no buildings large enough to serve as the courthouse. County officials carried out their business using whichever cabin or homestead was available to hold a brief meeting. The circuit court conducted its trials in a small log cabin.

In 1829, there still was no courthouse in Peoria. Court was held in a rented room on the second floor of a dry goods store. The county eventually bought the entire store and rehabbed the building to make it servable as a temporary courthouse.

In 1833 the county decided to build its first courthouse. The county clerk published a notice in several newspapers announcing that the county was in the market to buy 150,000 bricks. In 1834, the county hired Charles McClelan, a mason, to lay the bricks and George Macy, a carpenter, to install the framing and walls in the new courthouse. The temple-front style building was completed in the winter of 1836.

By the 1870s, after forty years of service, the old courthouse had become a tired building. In November 1875, the voters said yes to a bond issue to finance the construction of a new building. The firm of Wilcox and Miller, architects from Chicago, designed the county's second courthouse.

In 1962, that building was replaced by the current building. The firm of Lankton, Ziegele, Terry and Associates designed the present courthouse.

An Illustrated History | 117

Perry County

The section of the courthouse on the left was built in 1850 and the right in 1939. The middle portion was built in 1879.

Organized: January 29, 1827

County Seat: Pinckneyville

Named for: Commodore Oliver Hazard Perry

In 1828, Perry County built its first courthouse, an 18 by 22 foot, hewn-log structure that cost $54 (about $1,200 in 2007). The building's specifications called for a single door, one furnished with a good knob—not a wooden latch. One window was to be installed at the west end of the building and it was to have twelve 10 by 12 inch "lights" (window panes). The next year, workmen covered the logs with weatherboard and they set up a stray pen in a side yard.

In February 1836, despite an empty treasury and lack of support from citizens, the commissioners ordered work to begin on a new brick courthouse. Amos Anderson was the contractor for the 43-foot-square, two-story building. He finished his work in 1837, but received an I.O.U. for his pay. The county had to sell some of its surplus land to pay him and that took awhile.

118 | Illinois Courthouses

Above: The jail was built in 1871. It is located two blocks from the courthouse and is now used as a museum.

Right: An illustration in 1883 Combined History of Randolph, Monroe and Perry Counties *shows the courthouse with its 1879 addition. The smaller illustrations at the top of the page depict the County Farm for Indigents and the Jail.*

People kept forgetting to lock the courthouse door when they left of the evening. In 1840, the annoyed county commissioners hired a mechanic to put locks on the doors and windows "in such a manner as they would lock tight when closed and not be able to be opened from without." Hopefully, the locksmith installed the locks more in the spirit of the order rather than following the exact instructions.

On another occasion, the court wanted bids on a bridge construction project and their newspaper advertisement promised to award the contract "to the highest bidder."

In March 1849, over five hundred citizens petitioned the court to build a new courthouse. The court was quick to comply. By June, contractor Daniel W. Norris was at work constructing a 46 by 36 foot building. Norris's contract called for him to use the Roman "Tuscan order" for the masonry. That plain style is one of the five classic orders and considered the closest in style to the Greek Doric order. It was thought to convey the appearance of antiquity and strength to a building. The contract was completed on July 16, 1850.

In 1877, the county wanted to renovate the aged courthouse. The citizens rejected the court's request to sell bonds to finance the project. Newspaper stories cited the citizens' concern about the county's shaky finances and inability to repay the bond.

Stories that were printed a few weeks later told a different story. It seemed that a petition, allegedly signed by a majority of voters, was delivered to the commissioners asking them to ignore the negative vote and proceed with the remodeling project. Legal or not, public opinion obviously was in favor of moving forward. The court hired architect John Chapman of Du Quoin to draw up plans for a courthouse addition.

The 45 by 36 foot, two-story addition was connected to the old courthouse in 1879. William Wilson was the contractor and the cost was $9,742 (about $196,000 in 2007). The addition increased the width of the front of the structure to 81 feet.

An Illustrated History | 119

Piatt County

Organized: January 27, 1841

County Seat: Monticello

Named for: James A. Piatt, Sr., and John Piatt

Left: The dome remains on the 1903 Piatt County Courthouse but most of the interior rotunda space is now used to house an elevator shaft that was installed in 1958.

Below Top: The 1856 courthouse lost its cupola to a storm in 1871.

Below Bottom: The 1845 courthouse was a modest one-story building in the middle of the courthouse square. (Artist: Dale Summers)

Early court sessions at Monticello were held at the Devore Hotel. Whenever the court was not using the room, a tailor plied his trade there. Courthouse comedians liked to say that his suits hung together better than the ones presented by the lawyers. In 1845, the county built its first courthouse, a one-story, wood frame building. Furniture for the courthouse was made from walnut trees that grew nearby.

Not long after the courthouse was built, Illinois adopted a new constitution. One of the clauses in that 1848 document required newly elected officials to swear a new oath when they took office. In addition to a standard promise of fidelity to the peoples' welfare, elected officials henceforth had to swear on their sacred honor that they would not engage in fighting duels. It seemed that too many good men and bad were dying to make a point about the slavery issue.

In antebellum Illinois, a gentleman meeting another gentleman with a loaded pistol at dawn was considered a proper way to deal with an insult or disparaging remark. The authors of the 1848 Illinois Constitution hoped to put a stop to the nonsensical killings.

In 1856, the county built a two-story, brick courthouse. That building's cupola was destroyed during a storm in 1871 and never replaced. In 1900, the county officials wanted to build a new courthouse. The issue failed the first time it was considered by the voters but, in 1902, it was approved.

Architect Joseph W. Royer designed the building. The cornerstone for the structure was laid September 22, 1903. The citizens of Piatt County celebrated the building's centennial in 2003.

Pike County

Organized: January 31, 1821

County Seat: Pittsfield

Named for: Zebulon Pike, Santa Fe Trail Explorer

Right: The 1894 courthouse is octagonal, with dimensions of 110 by 119 feet. The dome's height is 136 feet.

Inset Right: A graceful curved dual spiral staircase surrounds the light well opposite the courtroom.

Below: The 1821 courthouse at Coles' Grove was the political center of northern Illinois when Pike County included one-third of the state's land surface.

Pike County came into being as a huge piece of real estate. In the following years, it was subdivided to create nine full counties and portions of several others. In 1821, Chicago (still called Fort Dearborn then) was located inside Pike County's borders.

The county's first county seat was at Coles' Grove, a town that was located on land that eventually became Calhoun County. Daniel Shin (or Shinn) built a 16 by 18 foot, hewn-log cabin to serve as the courthouse. He built the structure without using a single nail. In 1823, the county seat was relocated to a town called Atlas. Workmen took Shin's courthouse apart and dragged the logs to the new county seat and reassembled the building. Later, the county added a clerk's office and jail.

Pike County's boundaries were redrawn again in 1825 and Atlas lost its central location. By 1827, citizens began petitioning for a chance to select Pittsfield, a more convenient site, as the new county seat. For a time, those appeals fell on unresponsive ears. The tension for and against the relocation percolated for several years and was not decided until 1832 when the legislators authorized an election to settle the question.

Pittsfield was selected to become the new county seat. In 1833, Israel N. Burtt built a small, frame courthouse, but almost as soon as the building was completed it was decided that a larger, more ornate structure needed to be built. The frame structure was sold and used as a bakery and grocery for many years.

In 1836, work began on a replacement courthouse and it was completed in 1838. The court paid Benjamin L. Osborne $20 (about $450 in 2007) to draw plans for the building. In 1854, a "fireproof" office building was built near the public square.

The present courthouse was designed by architect Henry Elliott. Work began in 1894. Robert Franklin, a master stone carver, is remembered for creating much of the building's intricate stone work.

An Illustrated History | 121

Pope County

Organized: January 10, 1816

County Seat: Golconda

Named for: Nathaniel Pope, Territorial politician and jurist

The 1871 courthouse stands near the point where thousands of Cherokee crossed over the Ohio River during their deportation to reservations in Oklahoma. The route they followed is now known as the "Trail of Tears."

Thomas Ferguson's cabin was a busy place. He was one of the county commissioners and his parlor was the temporary county courthouse while the court held its first meetings there. His front porch doubled as the waiting room for clients waiting to ride the ferry he operated back and forth between Golconda and the Kentucky side of the Ohio River. Meanwhile, his wife, Sarah, was busy in the kitchen serving drinks and meals to their tavern customers who gathered around the big fireplace. He also was a senator in the Illinois Territory's General Assembly.

Ferguson was sentimental about his wife. In 1816, he founded a town near his homestead and ferry business. He named it Sarahville. The town became the county seat. Robert Scott built the first courthouse. His fee was $66.66 1/2 (about $1,100 in 2007). The half-cent coin was issued by the U.S. government from 1793 to 1857. It was worth about ten cents in modern purchasing power. Scott's courthouse was a 24 by 26 foot, hewn-log structure.

In 1817, Sarahville's name was changed to Golconda. That was the name of a city in India where the fabulous Hope Diamond was mined. Pope County's residents had turned up some promising mineral deposits and thought it couldn't hurt to adopt a lucky name. Sarah's reaction to this fickleness was not recorded in the county's records.

In 1833 the county built its second courthouse. Daniel Field donated land for the purpose and James Hankins started work on the building in 1831. For some reason, Hankins could not complete the task. He missed the completion date and still failed to finish it after receiving two extensions from the court. Field finally dismissed Hankins and finished the job himself. The courthouse served the county for many years.

Time, weather, and lack of maintenance take their toll on all buildings, however, and in 1870, David J. Baker, a circuit judge, refused to hold court there any longer because he was afraid it might collapse without warning. The judge may have exaggerated to make his point but, in 1871, the county hired the architectural firm of Young and Frick to design a new courthouse. Bonds totaling $28,000 were quickly sold. The bid of Yost and Laymen, contractors, was accepted as the best and lowest offer. The final cost of the project was $20,336.76 (about $335,000 in 2007) and was completed on May 5, 1873. The Pope County Courthouse at Golconda is one of the oldest courthouses in Illinois still in continuous use.

Pulaski County

Organized: November 3, 1843

County Seat: Mount City

Named for: Kazimierz Pulaski, War of Independence General

The 1912 courthouse at Mount City.

Water rose to the second floor level of the courthouse during the 1937 Ohio River flood.

In 1843, the General Assembly passed legislation that allowed Pulaski County to separate from Alexander County. In the process, Alexander County's public debt as well as the public treasury was divided between the old and new counties. The amount of debt and cash was divvied up based on their respective populations.

The town of Caledonia was selected as the county seat of Pulaski County. It took awhile before a courthouse could be built so the new county officials kept office "out of their hats," meaning office holders did business on the fly, tucking into their hats any legal papers handed them. The "office" literally was with an officer, even if an officer was not in his office.

A question arose over the legality of such "out of office" transactions. In 1845, the General Assembly stood behind the Pulaski County officials by declaring that the state would guarantee the legality of any official act performed at these "portable" offices.

In 1847, a courthouse was constructed at Caledonia. The legislature, still backing their friends in Pulaski County, agreed to guarantee a $600 loan that the county needed to finish construction on the building.

In 1861, only two months before the assault on Fort Sumter, the Pulaski County seat was relocated to Mount City. The new county seat was only a few miles from Cairo on the Ohio River. Fearing attack, county officials knew that Mount City was closer to the protection of federal troops who were thick in the area and busy beefing up Union defensive positions along the Mississippi and Ohio rivers.

The citizens of Mount City donated their city hall building to the county to serve as a courthouse. A fire in 1879 destroyed "the courthouse," but it is unclear if the building that burned was the old city hall or another building that had been constructed later. Virtually all of the county's records prior to 1860 were lost in that blaze.

In 1912, the county built the present courthouse. In 1937, the Ohio River overflowed its banks to create an epic path of watery destruction that devastated the land from Cincinnati to Cairo. Mount City was inundated and had to be evacuated. The courthouse was flooded, but survived and still serves.

An Illustrated History

Putnam County

Organized: January 13, 1825

County Seat: Hennepin

Named for: Israel Putnam, War of Independence General

The 1839 courthouse has been expanded several times, but the core building remains intact.

The "built in 1839" metal tag nailed to the wall is thought to have been placed by an Historic American Buildings Survey team during the 1930s.

Putnam County's original boundaries included most of the upper one-third of the state. Its "footprint" extended from Lake Michigan on the east, to the Illinois and Kankakee rivers to the south, to the Wisconsin line on the north, and stretched almost to the Mississippi River on the west. Reapportionment began in 1827 as new counties were formed and continued throughout the 1830s when its present borders were established.

Hennepin began as a trading outpost perched on the edge of that vast wilderness. White settlers were few in northern Illinois and they visited the small village to buy supplies, pick up mail, and trade furs. Eventually the town became the county seat.

The first circuit court met in the open air. When the first grand jury was empanelled, its members used a log as their bench. One of the first indictments they handed down was against a man charged with bigamy. A member of the jury said, "A man ought to be indicted for having two wives, when most of us haven't been able to get one."

About this same time, the county court authorized building a temporary courthouse but that order seems to have been rescinded or ignored. In June 1833, a new order was issued and a substanial wood frame building was built. The court also ordered construction of a jail. It was a hewn-log structure, twelve foot square, seven feet high, with a one foot square window. To the embarrassment of the court, the first prisoner held there, a man named Tallmadge, escaped rather easily when several of his friends kicked loose a few logs.

In 1837, the Illinois legislature passed an act "to establish and maintain a general system of internal improvements." The state took upon itself the task of building canals and railroads and came within an eyelash of bankrupting itself in the process. To secure passage of the bill the General Assembly had to allocate funds to all of the counties and about ten thousand dollars was sent to Putnam County's treasury. Unfortunately, the county invested in projects that were not self-sustainable and without additonal funds from the state they soon failed.

In 1839, the county built its present courthouse. The Greek-Revival style building was designed by J. A. Williams and built by the firm of Gorham & Durley. It is reckoned to be the oldest courthouse in Illinois still used for its original purpose. Additions have been added to the core building to increase office space.

The Plow that Opened the Prairie

In 1837, John Deere, a hardworking and ambitious Yankee blacksmith, moved to the Illinois frontier. A native Vermont man, he had established a reputation as a careful and inventive iron worker before trekking west.

Opportunity often appears with an unsmiling face, however, and thus it was so in Deere's case. The young blacksmith made good tools and was a respected smithy but his Rutland shop had to compete with a number of neighboring blacksmiths. Deere could not attract new customers fast enough to satisfy his creditors. Breaking even in Vermont, never mind becoming successful, had turned into a no-win struggle. Beaten but undaunted, he decided that it was time to seek out untapped opportunities on the frontier.

Artwork: Reviewing Performance – The Story of John Deere, *1936 by Walter Haskell Hinton. (Courtesy the John Deere Art Collection, Deere & Company, Moline, IL. USA)*

Deere sold his Vermont shop to his father-in-law and headed west. He opened his new shop at Grand Detour, a small village in Ogle County. This was rich, open land situated in the heart of the northern Illinois prairie. The Black Hawk War had ended a few years earlier and settlers were beginning to pour into the Indian's former buffalo hunting grounds.

Deere repaired tools and crafted the usual metal implements for the settlers. As he worked at his anvil shaping the hot iron, he listened to the farmers as they talked amongst themselves about how hard it was to plow the dark sticky soil. Furrowing the dirt, they said, was so tough that it took an oxen team just to slice through the hardpan. And, even then, the farmers complained, they still had to halt their teams every few feet to scrape the blade clean. The young blacksmith realized it was the old-style plow that the farmers were using that was the problem, and not the soil. Their old plows had traveled with them from their farms back east and proved to be ill suited for the hard-to-turn prairie. The opportunity to make a better plow had fallen into Deere's lap.

Deere went into his shop and began to work on the problem. After tinkering and testing several designs, he came up with a wrought-iron framed plow that had a polished steel share. It scoured itself clean as it cut the furrows and turned out to be ideal for the midwestern farmland. In 1838, Deere sold his new plow to a neighbor, Lewis Crandall. Word spread quickly and before long several other local farmers placed orders for a copy of Deere's marvelous plow. By 1841, Deere was manufacturing nearly one hundred plows per year. The impenetrable prairie had been conquered by a man with an idea and the talent to turn that idea into a reality.

Today, the John Deere Company, with headquarters at Moline, Illinois, provides farm equipment to an international market.

Randolph County

Organized: April 28, 1809

County Seat: Chester

Named for: Edmund Randolph

Above: The 1972 courthouse at Chester. An observation deck at the rear of the building provides visitors a view of the Mississippi River Valley below.

Inset Above: An illustration in the History of Randolph, Monroe and Perry Counties depicts the 1849 courthouse. The courthouse was razed but the jail is now used as a museum.

Randolph County was organized only a month after the United States government established the Illinois Territory. The town of Kaskaskia was the territorial capital and the county seat. Circuit court sessions were held at various taverns in the community but, in 1812, the county rented a house to act as a makeshift courthouse. In 1818, the same year that statehood was achieved, the county purchased it outright to use until a permanent courthouse could be built.

In 1819, the county issued a contract to J. W. Comley and his partner J. W. Nelson to build a brick, two-story courthouse. The contractors finished their work and turned the building over to the county for occupancy in 1821.

Right: Chester was the boyhood home of Elzie C. Segar, the man who created Popeye, the popular cartoon character. Popeye is the town's mascot and this six-foot-tall, 900-pound bronze statue of the spinach-eatin' sailor, sculpted by Robert Walker, was placed in the Segar Memorial Park in 1977 by the Chester Sorority Ladies. (Photo courtesy of Spinach Can Collectibles and the Official Popeye Fan Club, Popeye© King Features Syndicate.)

Below: An atrium fountain is at the base of the courthouse's five-story spiral staircase.

Like most towns along the Mississippi River, Kaskaskia endured periodic flooding. In 1847, high water turned the town into an island. The county government threw in the towel and began searching for a new site for the county seat. Several run-off elections were held to decide the issue. Kaskaskia's residents claimed the elections were structured, some yelled "rigged," to make sure their wet-footed town never had a chance. Eventually only two towns were left in the contest. The choice boiled down to the town of Sparta, farther inland, and Chester, a town a few miles down river but high and dry on a bluff that overlooked the valley.

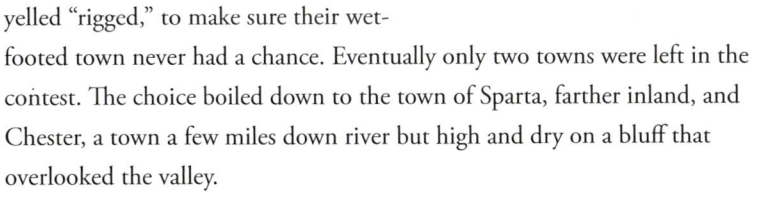

Chester became the new county seat. Several county officials refused to move to the new site, they were still loyal to Kaskaskia. Finally the circuit clerk complied, but the county recorder remained defiant. In 1848, the county commissioners declared the recalcitrant official's office "vacant" and he was ousted. Being drummed out of office did not tarnish his popularity, however. At the next election, the voters "triumphantly" re-elected him to his old office, albeit at the new location.

In 1849, William P. Haskins built the first courthouse at Chester. The building was paid for by private individuals. A jail annex was added in 1864. The old courthouse has been razed but the annex is used as the county's historical museum. The current courthouse was built in 1972. The architectural firm was Hanna, Breitweiser and McCaughlin.

An Illustrated History | 127

The 1914 courthouse at Olney.

Richland County

Organized: February 24, 1841

County Seat: Olney

Named for: Richland County, Ohio

In 1841, when a new county was established, the legislature expected that county to build a courthouse within two years to satisfy its charter requirements. That presented a problem for the folks who organized Richland County. The small population there could be taxed to the tune of about $200 per year. That was barely enough to pay the county's regular bills and far short of the kind of money that it would take to build even a modest courthouse. The county's other fundraising option was to sell some of the public land the county owned, but with few residents seeking to expand their holdings that looked like a slow and uncertain proposition. What to do?

128 | Illinois Courthouses

Left: The 1874 courthouse was destroyed by fire in 1913. (Artist: Ann Moehle)

Right: Work on the foursquare courthouse began in 1843 but was not completed until 1847. (Artist: Ann Moehle)

In 1841, the county came up with an ingenious, albeit, temporary solution. The Methodist Congregation in Olney had enough money to build a church but not enough to purchase land. The county decided to donate some public land to the church in exchange for the right to use the building as a courthouse during the week. The Methodists built a 20 by 24 foot, one-story building. The two entities shared the same building for a few years and the doctrine of separation of church and state, at least in this instance, appeared to have survived the ordeal.

In 1843, the county began work on a foursquare, frame courthouse with a cupola. The contractor underestimated the cost of the project and had to default midway through construction. The building sat idle for awhile. It was completed in 1847 by Asa Beard and Henry Spring. In 1859, a "fireproof" annex was built nearby to provide offices for the recorder and treasurer and to store records.

Architect J. C. Cochrane designed the 1874 courthouse. That neo-classical building featured an open tower, portico, and mansard roof. It was destroyed by fire on October 30, 1913. The present courthouse was constructed in 1914. J. W. Gaddis was the architect.

The 1841 courthouse was a church on Sunday and courthouse the rest of the week.

An Illustrated History | 129

Rock Island County

Organized: February 9, 1831

County Seat: Rock Island

Named for: Rock Island, an island in the Mississippi River

The 1896 courthouse as it appears today.

In 1831, Rock Island County's organizers held their early meetings in John Barrel's house at the village of Farmhamburg. Barrel's cabin also served as the local post office and public inn. It was officially designated as the temporary county seat in 1833.

In 1835, the General Assembly ordered a search to find a new site to serve as Rock Island's permanent county seat. The search committee visited several likely locations before recommending the town of Stephenson (later renamed Rock Island).

In 1836, the county bought 200,000 bricks for $1,600 (about $33,750 in 2007). Samuel Smith was hired to build the foursquare, two-story courthouse. Smith added a cupola and declared the project completed in December 1837.

That same year, the county built a hewn-log jail. It was expanded a few years later to provide living space for the sheriff and his family. The jailhouse expansion also added office space for the circuit clerk, recorder, and county clerk. Prudently, the county's tax receipts were stored in the treasurer's office, which was at a different location.

In 1882, a fire destroyed the combination jail and county office building. There was interest in building a new, larger courthouse to hold all of the county offices in one place but, in 1883, the county decided instead on a single-story, brick building for the displaced officials. S. J. Collins completed construction of the building in one year.

Entreaties continued for a new courthouse. The issue simmered for several years until 1894 when the county placed a bond issue before the voters. The electorate said "yes" to the sale of bonds valued at $125,000 (about $2,855,500 in 2007). Work on a new courthouse was finally underway.

The architectural firm of Gunn and Curtis provided the design. The cornerstone was set on October 1, 1896. During the twentieth century, the central tower and caps on the smaller twin towers that flank the entrance of the building were removed, along with several other roof line alterations.

The drawing shows the building as it looked before the tower and caps were removed from the roof. (Artist: Barry Kalinauskas)

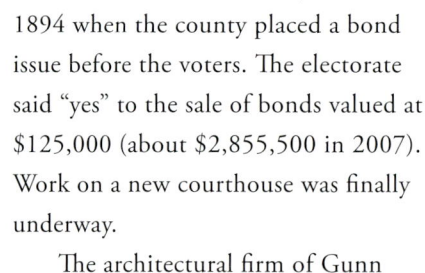

Left: In 1854, the Chicago and Rock Island Railroad completed its route between the Windy City and the Mississippi River. In 1856, the first railroad bridge over the Mississippi was completed at Rock Island, opening the way for the railroad to continue into Iowa and markets farther west. (Artist: William Gustafson)

130 | Illinois Courthouses

The 1967 courthouse.

Saline County

Organized: February 25, 1847

County Seat: Harrisburg

Named for: Salt springs in the area

In 1847, the General Assembly passed the enabling legislation to bring Saline County into existence. The passage of this bill was identical to the ones that created Illinois' other 101 counties, but unique because Abraham Lincoln was the Springfield lawyer who guided that particular piece of legislation over the legislative hurdles. Lincoln was the perfect choice since he had served many terms in the General Assembly himself, but was not currently a member of the body because he was serving his one term as a member of the U.S. House of Representatives.

More curious perhaps was the fact that Saline County was formed so late. From its earliest days, the area (even while still part of Gallatin County) was an invaluable contributor to the state's financial well being. In 1818, the heart of Illinois' salt production industry was located along the Saline River—whose all three forks ran through the county. The tax revenue that the state received from the sale of that salt almost single-handedly kept Illinois' financial head above water. Tax revenue from other industries such as mining, tobacco, and cotton farming eventually replaced the salt kettles, but that did not happen until the 1840s.

Saline's first county seat was at Raleigh between the years 1847 to 1859. Two courthouses were built in that community: a frame building in 1848 and a 36 by 40 foot, two-story, brick structure around 1854. In 1859, the county seat was moved to Harrisburg, a town closer to the geographical center of the county.

In 1860, the first courthouse built in Harrisburg was a Greek-Revival style building. The portico was supported by two central stone columns that were flanked by brick columns encased in plaster. J. K. Frick & Company architects prepared the plans and specifications.

That building was replaced in 1904. The new courthouse was a three-story building with a central bell tower. That courthouse was razed to provide space for the current courthouse.

In 1967, the present courthouse was constructed using the plans of the architectural firm of Clark, Altay & Associates.

The 1904 courthouse.

An Illustrated History | 131

Sangamon County

Organized: January 30, 1821

County Seat: Springfield

Named for: The Sangamon River

In 1821, two members of the county seat selection commission watched as the third member drove a stake in the ground to mark the spot where Sangamon County's town square would be located. A hewn-log courthouse was built on that spot at a cost of $84 (about $1,860 in 2007). The carpenter constructed the building as directed but improvements had to be made later in the year when the weather turned cold. Workmen added a fireplace and installed glass panes in the window to keep out the snow.

Above: The 1991 courthouse. The architects were Fisher—Wisnosky Architects, Inc.

Inset Above: The 1845 courthouse remained in service for about thirty years.

132 | Illinois Courthouses

Above: In the 1870s the old statehouse became the Sangamon County Courthouse. In 1899, shortly after this picture was made, a ground level, third floor was added. In 1961, by then a national historic site, the building was dismantled and rebuilt to its original two-story configuration.

In 1825, there was a proposal to build a brick courthouse that would have cost $3,000 (about $70,600 in 2007) but that idea sputtered and died when it attracted little support from the private donors who were being solicited to pay 50 percent of the cost. The court settled for a more modest frame building that cost only $519 (about $12,200 in 2007). Robert Thompson drew the plans for the building and was paid $2.25 (about $50 in 2007).

A third courthouse was built in 1831. It was a brick, foursquare, two-story, hip roof structure with a cupola. The timing of other events that took place soon after this building was finished created some heartburn. In 1837, while this structure was still new, the General Assembly was making plans to move the state capital from Vandalia to Springfield. Part of the deal for relocating at Springfield was that Sangamon County would turn over the land where the courthouse was standing to the state as the site for a new capitol. The city and county were eager to become the state capital so they agreed to surrender the land, vacate the courthouse, and pay $50,000 toward construction of the new statehouse.

The courthouse was razed and work began on the statehouse but, unfortunately, the destruction of the county building coincided with the financial crash of 1837. Rather then being able to build a new courthouse, the finanically strapped county had to rent space in a warehouse for the next ten years that was owned by local attorney Ninian W. Edwards. Edwards was the son of a former governor and a member of the "Long Nine," a group of state legislators (including Abraham Lincoln) who often banded together on legislative issues and masterminded the move of the capital from Vandalia to Springfield.

By 1845, the county's economy had recovered enough to build a replacement courthouse. It was a temple-front structure that remained in service for the next thirty years.

In 1867, the legislators decided to build a larger statehouse. Again, this deal required a land-swap agreement between Sangamon County and the state. The state's part of the deal was that the county would be the only entity allowed to buy the old statehouse. The county agreed to supply the state with land upon which to build the new structure and donate $200,000 towards the cost. The various elements of this agreement fell into place over time—seven years would pass before the county got the keys to the old statehouse— but, in 1876, it became Sangamon County's courthouse.

In the twentieth century, the former statehouse was purchased by the state and restored to pristine condition as a historic site and museum. The current Sangamon County Courthouse was built a few blocks away in 1991.

Schuyler County

Organized: January 13, 1825

County Seat: Rushville

Named for: Philip Schuyler, Founding Father

Above: E. O. Fallis was the architect for the 1880 courthouse. Its design was based on a similar looking courthouse that Fallis built a few years earlier for Monroe County in Michigan.

Inset Above: The courthouse as it appeared in 1882 before the spire was removed from the tower.

In 1825, Schuyler County established a temporary county seat at Beardstown, a small village on the banks of the Illinois River. No courthouse was built and the county seat was moved the next year to Rushton (later renamed Rushville). Beardstown remained out of the public eye for the next 170 years, until in the 1990s it received national attention as the hometown of a group of ladies who formed an investment club and published a best selling book called, *Beardstown Ladies' Common-Sense Investment Guide*.

Back in 1826, Rushville became the county seat and the county built a hewn-log courthouse there. Several years later, a jail and stray pen were added to the list of public buildings.

In 1829, a small office building was constructed for the county clerk. Later that same year, the county decided to expand the court's accommodations as well. William McCreery, a local stone mason, was hired and the foursquare style building he constructed was ready for occupancy in 1831. Sadly, McCreery was the first victim of a cholera epidemic that swept the town in 1834.

His sturdy courthouse served the county for half a century, requiring only the usual minor repairs. After the Civil War, there were petitions calling for construction of a new courthouse but each time an election was held the voters defeated the notion.

In 1880, on the third attempt, the proposal finally passed—but only by one vote. In 1881, the county perhaps mollified some of the opposition to the project by surrendering the public square to the town of Rushville for use as a city park. The county razed the old courthouse and work began on the replacement.

The 1829 courthouse. In 1837, the county paid $3.50 to bronze the ball on the weathervane atop the spire.

Architect E. O. Fallis was hired. The building committee liked the look of a courthouse Fallis had designed for the city of Monroe, the county seat of Monroe County in Michigan. They asked him to create a similar building for Schuyler County. Fallis did not consider this an unusual request; few politicians want to be on the cutting edge of architectural innovation. Contractor Thomas Keegan completed construction in the summer of 1882. The asymmetric tower was capped with a tall spire.

The Schuyler County Courthouse was renovated during the 1990s. With the exception of replacing the spire that had been damaged by a storm, the building was returned to its original splendor. County officials continue to take pride in pointing out that the restoration was accomplished at no cost to the taxpayers. They also point out that much of the credit for the success of the project should be given to an out-of-work roofer named Marty Trinkle and a perceptive circuit court judge named Carson Klitz.

Trinkle was facing time in the county jail and Klitz thought it would be better to have Trinkle work off his indebtedness to the county instead of sitting in a cell. Trinkle had no experience or training in the art of restoration but Klitz had faith in Trinkle's natural talent. Trinkle began by restoring the old courtroom.

During the 1970s, the courtroom ceiling had been lowered and fluorescent lighting installed. The modernization hid all of the charm and ambiance of the old building. Trinkle hand-cut stencils and painted the walls. He used old photos as a guide.

Local craftsmen got involved into the project as well. Herbert McCombs and Charles Crook, two local machinists, built a replacement chandelier for the courtroom. Israel Bauer's widow donated the old jurors' chairs. Israel had stored the chairs in his basement when the courtroom was re-done in the 1970s. The clock in the courtroom once hung in the office of former Circuit Clerk Harriett Hester. Youth offenders who appeared before Judge Klitz were given the opportunity to strip old paint from the banisters and woodwork throughout the building.

Today, the Schuyler County Courthouse shines like a new penny.

Left: Hand-cut stencils were used to reproduce the trim detail. The restoration was accomplished without tax money.

Right: Youth offenders stripped layers of paint from the stairs and banister in the courthouse.

Scott County

Organized: February 16, 1839

County Seat: Winchester

Named for: A local pioneer family

Scott County, formed from Morgan County, was established in 1839. The partition was not without controversy. Morgan County's negotiators gerrymandered the boundary line with Scott County to ensure that the farms that paid substantial taxes remained in their county. Scott County got more of the undeveloped land.

Three towns vied for the county seat honors: Manchester, North Prairie, and Winchester. Manchester was too far south and never considered a strong contender. North Prairie and Winchester, towns that were located only a few miles apart, were the main competitors. Winchester secured the county seat honor after agreeing to donate land for the courthouse square and pledging $5,000 toward construction of the county's first courthouse and jail.

Winchester had been platted in 1830 and was a well-established community by the time Scott County was formed. The first businesses in the town were a tannery and a dry goods store. The dry goods store sold whiskey at 6 and 1/4¢ a cup, which, according to legend, was ladled out of a tin container that previously had been filled with finely ground black pepper.

Winchester's favorite son was Stephen A. Douglas, a man who stood just over five feet tall and was nicknamed the "Little Giant." Douglas was only nineteen when he moved from Vermont to the community in 1833. During his first year in town he earned $120 (about $3,100 in 2007) for teaching school, and in his free time he studied the law. He soon gave up his teaching career and began a meteoric rise as lawyer, judge, and U.S. Senator.

In 1841, Scott County started building its first courthouse, a foursquare, two-story, brick structure. That is the year that Douglas was serving as an associate justice of the Illinois Supreme Court. Before Scott County's courthouse was completed, Douglas was elected to his first term as a member of the United States House of Representatives. He was not eligible to run for the Senate, the minimum age was thirty and Douglas was only twenty-seven.

In 1885, the county built its current courthouse. It was built on a corner lot a short distance from the old town square. That property was converted to a public park. James Stewart and Company furnished the plans and specifications for the building. The firm of Mathers, Buckingham and Zeigler of Jacksonville built the structure for $35,500 (about $750,000 in 2007). A tower clock was added in 1917.

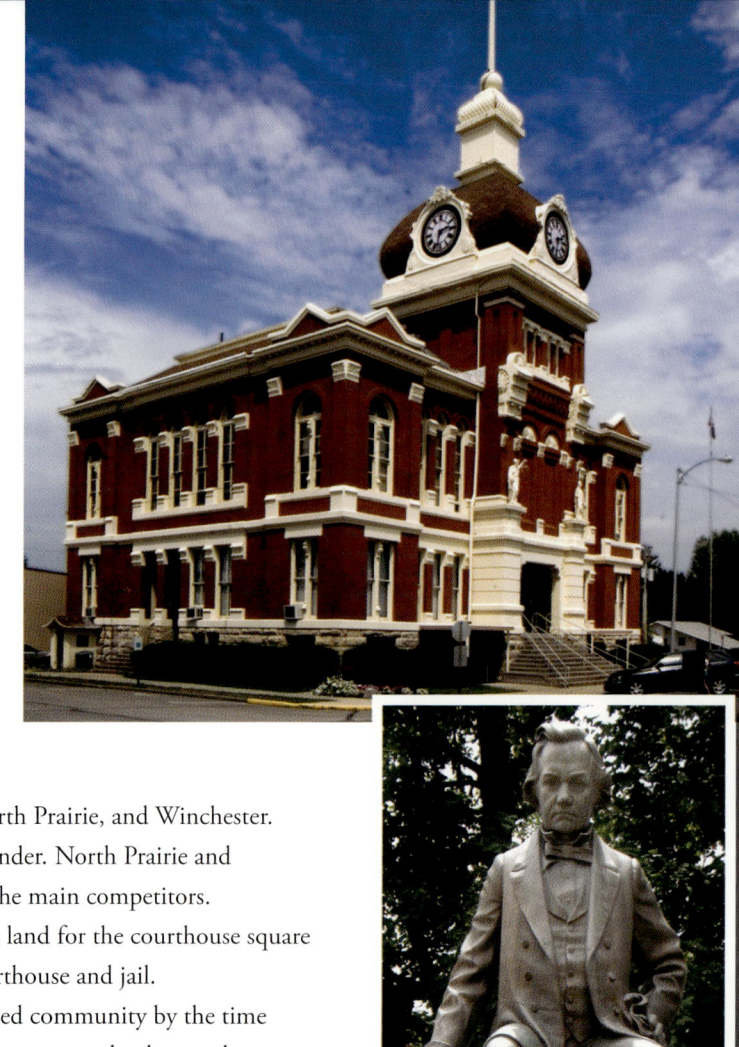

Above: The 1885 courthouse's onion-shaped dome was influenced by the Byzantine and Eastern religious architectural style that was popular at the time.

Inset Above: In 1930, a statue of the diminutive (he stood 5' 4") but powerful Stephen A. Douglas was erected in the Winchester town park. (Sculptor: Fred M. Torry)

136 | Illinois Courthouses

Shelby County

Organized: January 23, 1827

County Seat: Shelbyville

Named for: Isaac Shelby, Governor of Kentucky

One September morning in 1827, the newly appointed county commissioners met at the home of Barnet Bone. The first action they took that day was to order the construction of a courthouse. William Hall agreed to build it for $110 (about $2,500 in 2007). He finished in April 1828. The building was a 20 by 24 foot, hewn-log, two-story structure. The building had an outside set of stairs. Judges preferred exterior stairs so that people clumping up and down the steps to see county officials on the second floor would not have to pass through the courtroom.

In 1832, the county built its second courthouse, a foursquare building. Court records indicate that the building cost the county $1,094 (about $26,600 in 2007).

In 1881, construction was completed on the county's third and present courthouse. O. H. Placey was the architect. The county purchased 1,750,000 "hard" bricks from a local brick yard, paying $6 per 1,000. Labor and the other construction materials brought the total cost to $72,987.20 (about $1,440,000 in 2007).

Above Top: The 1879 courthouse. The tower clock came from the old Main Street School. When the school building was razed in 1928, the clock then was moved to the courthouse.

Above Middle: The 1827 courthouse. (Artist: Robert Root)

Right: The 1832 courthouse. The cupola was added in 1837.

An Illustrated History | 137

Left: A street view of the 1976 courthouse includes a covered walkway that connects the building with a parking garage.

Inset Above: The plaza side of the building includes a pool with fountains. The courthouse was designed by Hellmuth, Obata and Kassabaum, Inc.

St. Clair County

Organized: April 27, 1790

County Seat: Belleville

Named for: Arthur St. Clair, Governor of the Northwest Territory

St. Clair County was Illinois' first county. It was created even before there was an Illinois. The county was in existence for nineteen years before the Illinois Territory was created from the Northwest Territory in 1809.

The seventeenth-century French colonial town of Cahokia became part of the United States on July 5, 1778. The old courthouse there became the United States territorial courthouse and a major political center for the next twenty-four years. In 1801, William Henry Harrison, then the Indiana Territory governor, named the Cahokia courthouse the legal and governmental center of an area that extended to the Canadian border.

The 1860 courthouse was expanded in 1893 using plans by architects Bailey and Kroener. (Artist: Davis Gray)

The Cahokia courthouse inherited by the Americans had been built in 1716. It was built in the French style; that is with the logs set vertically instead of laid horizontally. That building was still standing in 1904. During the St. Louis World's Fair, some entrepreneurs moved it to the fairgrounds and used it as a concession booth.

By 1814, St. Clair County had decreased to its current size and the county seat was moved to Compton Hill (later renamed Belleville). The county proceeded to build a series of courthouses during the following decades, trying to keep pace with the county's expanding population.

In 1860, the county built its fifth courthouse. That building was considered the most historically significant of the series but it was razed in the 1960s. The destruction of the old building triggered a tussle of the first order between local preservationists, county officials, and the judiciary.

The building had been designed by architect Robert Mitchell and built entirely with materials from St. Clair County. The only exception were some stone floor tiles imported from Europe. By all accounts it was a handsome and popular local landmark.

Meanwhile, throughout the 1960s, the county's population increased. The county decided that the best way to provide more services would be to build a new courthouse. Preservationists were jolted into action when the news of the courthouse's pending destruction was announced in the media. But by then they were too late. Contracts had been signed and work was already underway. A law suit was filed and the matter was heard by a district court judge. He ruled that undoing the contracts at such a late date would damage the county's creditability to make future commitments. A headache ball smashed into the walls of the old courthouse on June 1, 1972. The current courthouse was completed in 1976.

The 1716 courthouse was cut down in size and used as a concession booth at the 1904 Worlds Fair at St. Louis. Abandoned, in 1906 it was moved to Jackson Park in Chicago. (Library of Congress: HABS photograph by Albert J. DeLong, circa 1934)

An Illustrated History | 139

Stark County

Organized: February 27, 1841

County Seat: Toulon

Named for: John Stark, Battle of Bunker Hill Commander

The 1856 Stark County Courthouse was built from the same set of plans that was used to build the 1853 Marshall County Courthouse.

Colonel William H. Henderson was a local political chieftain during the 1840s when Stark County was being organized. He picked "Toulon" as the name for the county seat. He liked that name because it was same name as a county in Tennessee, where he'd lived for many years before moving to Illinois. The decision of where to locate the county seat, after he'd selected its name, was made during a meeting held at his house. Subsequent court sessions were held in Henderson's parlor for the next several months, too.

In 1842, Abel Mott was hired to erect a frame courthouse on the public square. However, when he tried to turn the building over to the commissioners they refused to accept it, citing dire concerns about the quality of his work. The commissioners said it was not suitable and Mott argued with heat that the building was exactly what they had ordered when they hired him. The matter was settled through arbitration. Several citizens were asked to examine the building and give their objective opinion. The men said they thought the work looked like it was up to snuff and Mott was paid in full. That courthouse remained in service for nearly fifteen years.

In 1856, the county decided to build a new courthouse. The building committee heard favorable reports about a smart looking Greek-Revival courthouse that had been built in Marshall County three years earlier. Several of the men rode over to Lacon and liked what they saw there.

They secured a copy of the Lacon courthouse plans and rode back to Toulon. And so, the present Toulon courthouse looks to be a copy of the 1853 courthouse that once stood at Lacon. In 1883, the county added a "fireproof" annex next to the core building for storage and additional office space.

Stephenson County

Organized: March 4, 1837

County Seat: Freeport

Named for: Benjamin Stephenson, prominent pioneer

Above: A 30-foot tall Civil War monument looms over the low profile silhouette of the 1974 courthouse.

Below: The 1865 courthouse was a community landmark after nearly 110 years on the courthouse square. Preservationists fought to stop its demolition but their request for an injunction was denied and the old building passed into history.

The 1837 courthouse was well-built and served the county for forty years.

Stephenson County's 1837 boundary lines were the result of many divisions and subdivisions that went on around its borders. In 1818, the county was divided almost equally between two mega-counties, Bond and Madison. As those two counties were reduced and new counties were formed, Stephenson County emerged.

In 1837, several towns from various corners of the county vied to be named as the county seat. The prime contenders were Cedarville and Freeport.

At the time, Cedarville was only a "paper" town. Suitable land was owned by speculators, but they were hesitant to invest in having the land surveyed and platted before learning if it would be selected as the county seat. Ethereal as it was, Cedarville did have the advantage of being located at the geographic center of the county.

Freeport, on the other hand, was an established town. It was only a few miles south of the Cedarville location and the town had a functioning saloon and a few other buildings. The speculators who owned Freeport also put an attractive offer on the table. They promised a cash bonus, land upon which to build a county building, and a free lot for each member of the committee charged with recommending the location of the county seat.

To the surprise of none, Freeport became the county seat.

In December 1837, the county hired Thomas J. Turner to build a frame courthouse and hewn-log jailhouse. Turner prepared the lumber and logs during the winter months and began construction in the spring. He finished the courthouse in 1840 and it served its purpose until it was razed in 1870 to make way for construction of a new building.

The 1865 courthouse, which featured elements of the "Second Empire" style, was a Freeport landmark for nearly 110 years. The old structure was added to the National Register of Historic Places, but it was too costly to maintain and inadequate for the mission for which it was built. Despite efforts by local preservationists, the courthouse was demolished in 1974.

The current courthouse was erected on the site in 1974. The plans and specifications for the building were provided by the firm of Johnson, Kile, Seehausen and Associates.

Pekin's 1916 courthouse is the second one constructed there. The first one was built in 1850 when Pekin reclaimed the county seat honor.

Tazewell County

Organized: January 31, 1827

County Seat: Pekin

Named for: Lyttleton Waller Tazewell, Governor of Virginia

In 1827, Tazewell County's first county seat was at Mackinaw, a town located at the geographic center of the county when its original boundary lines were drawn. The first courthouse was a one-and-half-story, hewn-log, 24 by 18 foot building.

Creating a contract was less formal on the frontier than it is today. The agreement made between the county and Amasa Stout to build a courthouse became official when the county clerk "cried out" that his bid had been accepted. Stout was the low bidder at $125 (about $2,800 in 2007).

The county held an auction to raise money for the construction. George Hittle, a surveyor's assistant, was hired to stake out the lots that would be put up for sale. He was paid $1.50 (about $35 in 2007). He got another $1.25 from the county treasury to cover the cost of the whisky that he ladled out free of charge to the prospective buyers who gathered to bid on the property.

Right: The Tremont Courthouse featured a square tower topped with a rounded cap.

Below Top: The crawl space under the Mackinaw courthouse provided a shady spot for stray pigs.

Below Bottom: In approximately 1849, a new courthouse was built, however, it was razed in 1914 for the current building.

In 1828, the courthouse was finished and occupied. The building's foundation allowed a few feet of crawl space and stray hogs liked to crawl underneath the building for a snooze. After a rain shower, the pigs enjoyed nothing more than a lazy rest in the wet goop, grunting contentedly while the lawyers conducted their business in the courtroom over their heads. If the boorish squeals threatened to overwhelm the court's proceedings, the judge would halt the trial while the lawyers crawled under the floorboards and drove off the hogs.

In 1831, Tazewell County was reduced in size. This changed the geographic center of the county. Pekin, a town on the Illinois River, became the new county seat. Instead of building a courthouse, a schoolhouse was pressed into service as a temporary courtroom and office space was rented at a tavern and other local buildings.

In 1836, Tremont, a town located about ten miles to the east, used Pekin's failure to build a courthouse to convince legislators that the county seat should be moved. Tremont's city fathers sweetened their offer by donating twenty acres and pledging $2,000. The county used this land and money to build a temple-front courthouse. The county seat remained at Tremont until 1850.

Pekin's residents may have been slow about erecting a courthouse when they first had the chance but they still had ambitions of being the county seat. In 1843, they tried to reclaim the honor but were defeated in that election. Their zeal was dampened further when scarlet fever claimed more than fifty lives in the community. The election and illnesses blunted their general interest in reclaiming the county seat for awhile, but, in 1849, the question was again placed on the ballot, and this time Pekin was successful.

Lesson learned, the Pekin citizens wasted no time in building a courthouse. It was a Greek-Revival style building with six columns to support its impressive portico.

That building was razed in 1914 to make way for the present courthouse. The turn of the century building that now stands on the public square was designed by the architectural firm of Deal and Ginzel.

An Illustrated History | 143

Union County

Organized: January 2, 1818

County Seat: Jonesboro

Named for: Second "Great Awakening" Religious Unity

Jonesboro was surveyed and platted in March 1818, only two months after the enabling legislation for Union County was passed by the General Assembly. Even as the surveyor placed his marker stakes, the young town was named as the county seat. The town was built on land donated to the county by John and Juliet Grammar. The exact date of the construction of the first courthouse is unknown, but probably soon after Jonesboro was selected since that was one of the requirements for being named as a county seat. The rustic 20 by 20 square foot structure was built by Thomas Cox. He used round logs. The floor was dirt with loose planks laid upon the ground. Sunlight came through one door and one window. The roof was clapboard. There were two rooms: the larger was the courtroom with a judge's bench as the single piece of furniture, and a smaller one served as a jurors' room.

Union County residents defended their rough looking courthouse. They insisted the justice that was administered in their plain building was just as good as the kind that came from a courthouse that cost half a million dollars.

In 1820, the county invested in a new frame courthouse that was erected in the middle of the public square. In 1838, that courthouse was replaced by a third building, a structure that quickly fell into disrepair either through shoddy workmanship or neglect. In 1858, it was razed and replaced by the current courthouse.

In 1854, the Illinois Central Railroad built a line through the county and the engineers planned to lay track through Jonesboro. To facilitate that route, the town was supposed to provide the railroad with a survey that would show the right of way but for some reason that was not done. Undoubtedly there was some other "horse trading" involved in the transaction that has since been forgotten. In any case, the city's survey failed to materialize. Instead, Winstead Davie submitted an alternate survey of a route that ran through his property, a mile east of Jonesboro. The Illinois Central adopted Davie's plan and bypassed the county seat. The railroad town of Anna, named for Davie's wife, was established and benefited accordingly.

In 1963, matching two-story wings covered with rough stone were added to the 1858 courthouse.

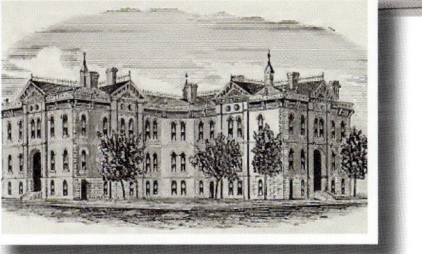

Above: The 1910 courthouse.

Inset Above: The 1876 courthouse.

Vermilion County

Organized: January 18, 1826

County Seat: Danville

Named for: The Vermilion River

The windswept, tall-grass prairie of east-central Illinois was one of the last regions of the state developed by settlers. The pioneers who arrived early in the state's development preferred the southern one-third of the state with ample forests and river access. Vermilion County attracted only fur trappers who lived amongst the Native American tribes and bands of hardy salt makers who extracted that precious commodity from the saline streams west of Danville.

During the 1830s, however, some ranchers began herding cattle there and discovered the endless grasslands provided ideal grazing. By 1835, great herds of cattle were being fattened before being shipped east. By the 1870s, the ranchers had switched to corn and were raising succulent, purebred beef cattle. Vermilion County was at the center of that ranching tradition. It was the home of famous ranches and millionaire cattle kings. Danville's cattle barons were supplying beef to the storied Chicago stockyards decades before the ranchers in the west stepped onto the stage.

The county's first courthouse, a sixteen-foot-square log structure, was constructed in 1827 and served for only three years. In December 1830, the county board posted notices in the local newspapers that they wanted to receive bids from contractors to build a new brick courthouse. The request generated scant interest, however, and it took a year before there were competitive bids. Work on the courthouse finally got underway early in 1832. Guerdon S. Hubbard was the contractor. He had the bricks made at a brickyard located on a nearby farm that had clay deposits. Hubbard's foursquare, two-story courthouse remained in use for nearly forty years. It was destroyed by a fire in 1872.

In 1876, construction of the new courthouse posed a challenge for Detroit architect E. E. Myers. He not only had to create a building with a large number of rooms, but he had to fit it onto an irregular patch of ground. The land available for the county's third courthouse had been donated to the county in 1827 and it was shaped like a private's chevron turned sideways.

The county's fourth and current courthouse was erected in 1910 on the same plot of ground as Myers's building. Architects C. M. Lewis and L. F. W. Stuebe took their cue from their predecessor and the general shape of their building resembled the earlier courthouse.

An Illustrated History | 145

Wabash County

Organized: December 27, 1824

County Seat: Mount Carmel

Named for: The Wabash River

In 1821, before Wabash County was divided from Edwards County, the town of Palmyra served as the county seat. Around that time, several families arrived from Great Britain and settled along the western edge of Edwards County. The expatriates persuaded the state legislature to relocate the county seat at Albion, a town near their homesteads. The Palmyra residents who lived near the Wabash River on the other side of the county considered this an unpatriotic move.

Bias against the British was still strong in the decade following the War of 1812. The Palmyra folks, whose roots were a few generations deeper in the soil of the new land, raised a militia to reclaim the county records from Albion and return them to Palmyra. Fortunately, no blood was shed. In 1824, when it became clear that neither camp would stop bickering over the county seat location, the state legislature split the difference and created Wabash County.

Above: The courthouse has been remodeled during its seventy-eight years to the point where no trace of the 1881 structure remains.

Inset Above: In 2007 workers cleaned and reset the county's war memorial near the front of the courthouse.

146 | Illinois Courthouses

Left: The second courthouse was built in 1831. It was destroyed by a fire in 1857.

Right: The third courthouse was built in 1857. It was destroyed by a tornado in 1877.

The Wabash County commissioners selected Centerville as the county seat. That town also was on the Wabash River but situated on higher ground than Palmyra. A log courthouse was constructed there in 1826. Within a few years it became clear that Centerville was not thriving and, by 1829, it was abandoned as a failure. The county seat was moved to Mount Carmel, an already prospering town at the time. Palmyra and Centerville vanished in time.

In 1831, Scoby Stewart built the county's second courthouse. It was a foursquare, two-story building that was destroyed by a fire in 1857. Virtually all of the county's records were lost in the blaze.

To reproduce the county's official records the county clerk copied personal copies of wedding licenses, property deeds, and other documents kept by residents. In 1871, that practice was followed on a much larger scale after the Great Chicago Fire destroyed Cook County's records. The General Assembly passed the "Burned Records Act" to protect county clerks who used personal documents to replace lost official copies. Generations of Illinois citizens since that time have carefully saved personal copies of their deeds, titles, and licenses, just in case.

The 1857 courthouse, built by Hiram Bell, also was destroyed by nature—a tornado in 1877. Mount Carmel's business center also was decimated. In 1881, the state allocated $15,000 to the county in disaster relief to help build a new courthouse. That building was extensively remodeled in 1959 and again in 1963. No trace of the core building remains.

The 1881 courthouse has been remodeled over the years to become the building seen today.

An Illustrated History | 147

Warren County

Organized: January 13, 1825

County Seat: Monmouth

Named for: Joseph Warren, War of Independence General

In 1825, Warren County's commissioners met at the county seat at Oquawka, a town on the Mississippi River that was inconvenient for folks living in the interior of the county. Court cases, on the other hand, were conducted by a circuit court that sat in Peoria County, far to the east and equally problematic for all.

In 1830, a court was established at Oquawka, which allowed cases to be adjudicated closer to home, but residents of the eastern half of the county still were discontented because the county seat was at Oquawka. The river town was the most heavily populated town in the county at the time, however, and its citizens were in no hurry to relinquish the honor of being the county seat.

In 1831, despite protests from Oquawka, a sort of a satellite courthouse was built in Monmouth. That building was replaced by a second ad hoc courthouse in 1835. The dispute over the location of the county seat reached a slow boil.

Finally, the members of the General Assembly got involved. Legislators rolled up their sleeves and log rolling ensued. In 1836, President Andrew Jackson issued a federal land patent to enlarge Warren County's size by giving it some land taken from the old federal Military Tract. That transfer offset the loss of land that Warren County experienced when Henderson County was created in 1841. Oquawka became Henderson's county seat. Monmouth became Warren County's seat of justice. Whoo!

In 1836, with Warren County's county seat question put to rest, the county issued an order for construction of a new, larger, foursquare style courthouse at Monmouth. They purchased a site for the building from Theodore Coburn for $1,000 (about $23,000 in 2007). There were delays, however, and the building was not finished until 1841.

One of the first cases to be heard in that courthouse was to decide if the Mormon leader, Joseph Smith, should be extradited to Missouri to stand trial for murder. Stephen A. Douglas was the judge. Smith was alleged to have been involved in several killings that escalated into a virtual war between the Mormons and the Missouri Militia. Douglas ruled that Smith should not be forced to return to Missouri to stand trial.

In 1893, work began on the present courthouse. It was completed in March 1895. Architect Oliver P. Marble drew the plans.

The 1893 courthouse tower used to be a taller structure with a spire that housed a clock and bell. That section was removed from the tower in 1970, supposedly to reduce the tower's weight on the building.

The 1836 courthouse briefly stood next to the present courthouse. The old building was razed soon afterwards.

148 | Illinois Courthouses

The 1884 courthouse as it appears today.

Washington County

Organized: January 2, 1818

County Seat: Nashville

Named for: George Washington

In 1818, the county seat of Washington County was at the town of Covington. The honor was something of a consolation prize. Covington, along with Carlyle and Vandalia, had been on the short list to become the new state capital the year that Illinois was admitted into the Union. But it was not to be and on August 20, 1818, Kaskaskia, the old territorial capital, was picked as a placeholder until the state government could be moved to Vandalia the following year.

Covington's county seat honor likewise was short lived. In 1824, Clinton County was established and that action shifted Covington to a spot on the northern-most edge of Washington County. A courthouse had been built there but the inconvenient location meant it was no longer tenable as the county seat. In 1831, a new town called Nashville became the county seat and the Covington courthouse was abandoned. The brickwork has disintegrated and no trace of the building remains.

On June 25, 1831, the county hired Thomas Moore to build a frame courthouse on the public square in Nashville. That building continued in use until it was razed early in 1840 to make way for construction of a new courthouse. The dimensional shape of the building is unknown but records indicate that the courtroom was on the ground floor and offices were on the second floor. Later, the arrangement was reversed and the courtroom was moved to the upper floor. The structure was destroyed by a fire in 1883.

As soon as the ashes from the fire cooled, the board of supervisors met in an emergency session in October 1883 and awarded a contract to A. Hollenbeck for construction of the current courthouse. The building was completed in 1884 at a cost of $23,999 (about $497,000 in 2007).

Twin one-story wings were added in 1965 to increase the office and storage space. During the construction of the addition, great care was taken to duplicate the key stones over the windows and match the color of the original bricks and limestone used for the addition's quoins and foundation stonework.

An Illustrated History | 149

Wayne County

Organized: March 26, 1819

County Seat: Fairfield

Named for: General "Mad" Anthony Wayne

Wayne County's first courthouse was a log building that was built on the public square sometime after 1819. That building was replaced by a two-story, foursquare type courthouse in 1836.

In 1840, young lawyer Abe Lincoln electioneered for William Henry Harrison's presidential candidacy on the lawn outside of the Wayne County Courthouse. To warm up his audiences, the long-legged Lincoln liked to challenge local men to jumping contests, which he usually won. The stake that marked the length of one of his jumps supposedly remained for years on the courthouse square. Harrison won the presidency for the Whig Party but died after only thirty-two days in office.

The 1836 courthouse served its purpose for over fifty years but, during the 1860s, officials started to worry about the safety of the county's records. For protection, the county built a separate "fireproof" building on the southwest corner of the square. Ironically, fire destroyed that building in 1886 and most of the records were lost in that blaze.

Meanwhile, vacant office space in the courthouse was rented to lawyers and businessmen. During the building's final years, the community was mortified to learn that a barbershop was being operated in the courthouse offices.

In 1891, a courthouse building committee approved plans for a new building. The blueprints called for it to be thirty-two feet from foundation to eave and the top of the spire would reach 128 feet. The clock tower would be placed over the entrance rather than from the center of the building. The building cost $24,700 (about $550,000 in 2007).

During the 1930s, the tower would be the scene of a stunt that nearly proved fatal to a young man by the name of Frank "the Human Fly" Kirby. People did ridiculous things for money during the Great Depression and Kirby was hired to climb the courthouse tower, the tallest building in the community. Unfortunately, as the crowd watched in horror, Kirby lost his grip and fell. He was seriously injured but lived. His plan, he said from his hospital bed, was to work his way up to heights such as the recently completed Empire State Building in New York City, at 1,250 feet the tallest building in the world at the time. After his injury at Fairfield, however, Kirby wisely retired from the daredevil business.

A new addition was added to the south side of the courthouse in 1955 and on the north side in 1957. Based on old photographs, it appears the cap on the tower's tapered steeple was shortened sometime during the twentieth century.

The 1891 courthouse as it appears today. Matching wings were added to the front of the building in the mid-1950s. An elevator was installed in 1997 and the courtroom was renovated in 2000. In the lower left of this photo is a plaque commemorating the Wayne County Republican's endorsement of Abraham Lincoln for president. The Wayne County men pledged their support in March, two months before the 1860 convention at Chicago where Lincoln was nominated.

White County

Organized: December 9, 1815

County Seat: Carmi

Named for: Leonard White, pioneer and early politician

Above Top: The 1883 courthouse as it appears today.

Above Right Inset: The 1828 courthouse also was used as the town's meeting place and social hall.

Above Inset: The tower over the entrance was removed and other roof line modifications were made during the twentieth century.

White County's first court was held at the home of John Craw. Built in 1814, it is Carmi's oldest house. It was later purchased by John Robinson, a U.S. Senator and Illinois Supreme Court Justice. Robinson's descendants lived there until the 1960s. It is now a museum.

In 1819, a frame courthouse was constructed but that building was "blown down" before 1824, presumably by a severe storm. Court sessions were again held at the Craw house. The county's elected officers also conducted business from their homes.

The first brick courthouse was erected in 1828 by Allen Rudolph. It was a two story, foursquare building with hip-roof and a square cupola. The first floor courtroom in the courthouse was the scene of religious and political meetings and town gatherings. When court was not in session, citizens met there to dance the Virginia reel, hold talent shows, and stage theater productions.

The current courthouse building was erected in 1883 on the same site as the previous building.

The Robinson-Steward home, formerly the Craw home, is now owned by the White County Historical Society.

Whiteside County

Organized: January 16, 1836

County Seat: Morrison

Named for: Samuel Whiteside, pioneer, political figure, and military leader

Above: The current courthouse in Morrison was erected in 1982–1987. The firm of Phillips, Swager & Associates designed the structure.

Inset Left: The 1863 Morrison courthouse was 85 by 55 feet, with a 75 foot high, domed cupola. The courtroom was a curved room with a balcony for spectators. The building cost $14,668.80 (about $207,000 in 2007).

The contest in Whiteside County to pick a site for the county seat was a protracted affair. Five elections were held in 1839 just to narrow the field. The eventual winner of that round was the town of Lyndon. Court sessions already were being held there and the town constructed a courthouse in 1840.

Nevertheless, the owners of the town of Sterling, one of the contenders, did not back down from their desire to have their town named as the county seat. They called for a recount of the votes. To Lyndon's dismay, the recount showed that Sterling had won an earlier contest by eleven votes. The county seat location was switched to Sterling. In 1842, the commissioners contracted with Luther Bush to build a two-story, foursquare, 40 by 40 foot, brick and stone courthouse.

Court continued to be held at Lyndon while the Sterling courthouse was being built but, in 1844, sessions commenced at the new county seat. Meanwhile, Lyndon's proprietors did not go quietly into the night. Their petition for a review of the recount eventually found favor within the legislature. In short time, the results of the previous recount were reversed. Lyndon had been the voters' chosen spot all along.

Sterling would have none of it. For the next four years, the county's administrative business was conducted in Lyndon but circuit court sessions continued to be held at Sterling. This stand-off lasted until 1847 when the General Assembly again dubbed Sterling as the "official" county seat.

That undisputable, irrevocable, and everlasting decision lasted until 1857. In that year, the legislature again authorized an election to decide the location of the county seat. In a surprise move, Sterling and Lyndon, the front runners, were upset by a dark horse. The town of Morrison was selected as the new county seat. It had the winning combination of being centrally located and situated on a major railroad line.

The first courthouse at Morrison was built in 1863 by John McKay.

Will County

Organized: January 12, 1836

County Seat: Joliet

Named for: Conrad Will, a Jackson County politician

The base of the 1969 courthouse features a 45 degree cantilevered buttress made of pre-stressed concrete. The building's design continues to attract comment.

Prior to 1836, while settlers first began moving into the area, Will County was divided between Cook County to the north and Iroquois County to the south. Within a few years, both of those larger counties were reduced to their present size by the formation of DuPage, Lake, McHenry, and Kankakee counties. The population continued to expand southward from Cook County and Will County was established.

A large part of the population growth could be traced to the workers being hired to build the Illinois and Michigan Canal. The route along the canal's path towards LaSalle became dotted with worker camps and settlements. The ninety-six-mile-long canal opened for traffic in 1848 and became a vital water link between the Great Lakes and the Gulf of Mexico. The construction of the Illinois Central Railroad system a few years later further underscored the area's importance as a major transportation hub. Both the canal and the railroad ran through the heart of Will County and Joliet.

In 1836, Will County's first circuit court was held in a rented room on the second floor of Wilson's Store. One day, when a grand jury hearing was scheduled to begin, the jury was short of a quorum they needed to proceed. The sheriff was instructed to "draft" the first five men he saw loitering on the street. He did and court continued.

The first courthouse in Joliet was constructed in 1837 and it stood until 1848. It was razed to make room for a new courthouse. The 1848 courthouse served its purpose until 1884. Construction of the third courthouse, designed by architect J. C. Cochrane, began in 1884. It was replaced by the present building in 1969.

The 1884 courthouse was razed in 1969. The outline of the building's foundation is still visible on the grounds behind the current courthouse.

An Illustrated History | 153

The lack of windows promotes energy efficiency in the 1971 courthouse.

Williamson County

Organized: February 28, 1839

County Seat: Marion

Named for: Williamson County, Tennessee

Williamson County was formed from Franklin County, one of the fifteen counties in existence in 1818 when Illinois achieved statehood. The men of Franklin County gathered at Garrett's Tavern to vote on whether or not to adopt the state's new constitution. The voting process then was different from the secret ballot used today. Then, when a man stepped forward to cast his vote, he announced his yea or nay in a loud voice. His vote was repeated aloud by the sheriff and then recorded. The constitution was adopted.

After Franklin County was subdivided in 1839 to create Williamson County, the commissioners chose the small settlement of Poor Prairie (later renamed Marion) as the county seat. The court held its early meetings in the clerk's office. The first public building constructed by the county was a log structure completed in 1839. That building served for only a few months.

In 1841, John Paschal built a two-story, 40 by 40 foot, brick, foursquare courthouse. The county outgrew that building, however, and in 1858, a contract was issued to Robert M. Hundley to construct a 50 by 70 foot, two-story, brick building.

That building was destroyed by a fire in 1875 but, fortunately, most of the county's records were saved. The property was sold. Without a home, court was held in rented quarters for the next ten years. In 1885, the county managed to pass a tax to create a building fund and soon collected enough to begin building a new courthouse.

Charles E. Brush completed the county's third courthouse in 1889. Four, one-story additions were added to the corners of the building in 1939. The work was financed by a Works Progress Administration grant. The building was painted white in 1945.

The present energy efficient courthouse was erected in 1971. Heat energy from the overhead lights is recycled to provide about 60 percent of the warmth needed during cold weather. The firm of Clark, Altay and Associates provided the plans and specifications for the 36,000 square foot building.

The bell tower part of the 1889 building was preserved and is on display in the town square. The building was painted white during the 1940s.

154 | Illinois Courthouses

Winnebago County

Organized: January 16, 1836

County Seat: Rockford

Named for: The Winnebago Tribe

Above: The Winnebago Criminal Justice Center.

Inset Above Right: The 1875 courthouse. Collapse of the tower during construction caused great loss of life.

Inset Above: The most recent courthouse was built in 1968 in downtown Rockford. (Photograph by Eugene Gamble)

The 1916 courthouse.

In 1836, the three members of the site selection committee reported to the General Assembly that the town of Winnebago was their choice to become the county seat. The county's elected commissioners rejected that pick because Charles Reed, one of the owners of the prospective site, wanted assurances that his thirty acres would be refunded if the county seat was ever moved to a new location. Reed's caution soured the deal. The elected officials wanted nothing short of a clear title.

For the next few years court sessions were conducted at various locations, including the house of Daniel S. Haight—the place where the county's organizational meetings had been held.

The proprietors of Winnebago meanwhile crafted one proposition after another that would result in the town being selected as the county seat, while still protecting their interests. All of their efforts were rejected. Finally, in 1839, a countywide election was held to determine which town should be named as the county seat. The town of Rockford won by a wide margin. (Too wide a margin some claimed because there were several hundred more Rockford votes counted in that election than in later elections.)

In 1841, a frame building was built in Rockford to serve as a temporary courthouse. A permanent courthouse was built in 1844. That structure was built by Derastus Harper and John Beattie. It was a one-story, 56 by 35 foot, brick building of the Classical-Revival style. In 1851, a fireproof stone building was erected nearby to store the county records.

In 1875, the county ordered the construction of a new courthouse. That building, designed by Henry L. Gay, suffered the catastrophic fate of collapsing before it was completed. The weight of the tower crushed the bricks in the support walls. The collapse killed nine men and wounded twelve others. In 1877, a coroner's jury found Gay guilty of incompetence for failing to properly take into account the weight of the tower in his plans. Work resumed and the building was completed in 1878.

The 1897 courthouse was restored and remodeled in 1981 by the firm of Landes, Benson, Parkins - Architects and Engineers.

Woodford County

Organized: February 27, 1841

County Seat: Eureka

Named for: Woodford County, Kentucky

Woodford's first county seat was at Versailles; placed there on a temporary basis until such time as an election could be held. Despite the provisional nature of the appointment, time passed and a courthouse was constructed there and the court held regular sessions. Fearing a fait accompli was afoot, other towns began to ask pointedly about when a permanent site for the county seat would be named.

An election to decide the issue was proposed, but that plan was scrapped. Instead, the legislators appointed five special commissioners to make the decision—always a good way to bring political maneuvering into the process—and the committee picked the town of Hanover (later renamed Metamora). A Classical-Revival style courthouse was constructed at Metamora and court sessions were held there beginning in September 1843. The town of Roanoke contested the choice in 1844 because there had not been an election, but the complaint was rejected.

The decision not to hold an election continued to rankle. Metamora remained the county seat for over fifty years, but following the Civil War, there were frequent contests attempting to move the county seat elsewhere.

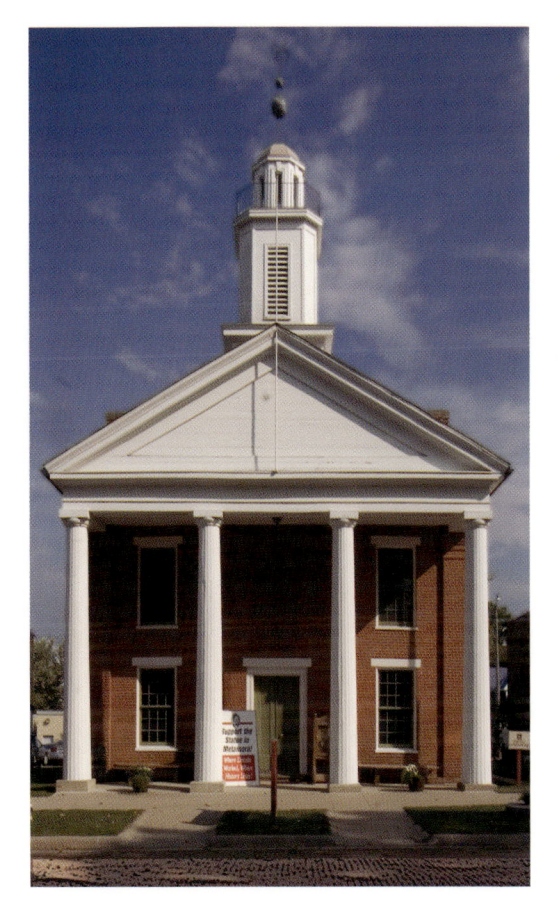

The Metamora courthouse is a state historic site. Abraham Lincoln and Adlai Stevenson, Sr., (Grover Cleveland's vice president) practiced law in this building before they were elected to national office.

In rapid succession the towns of El Paso (1867), Eureka (1869), and Roanoke (1873) each stepped forward to vie with Metamora to be named as the county seat. In 1894, Eureka challenged for a second time and was successful at the ballot box. Even so, Metamora balked and it wasn't until an Illinois Supreme Court ruling in 1896 validating the election results that the change took place.

Eureka moved promptly to construct a courthouse. In 1897 the county commissioners selected the firm of Bell and Kent to design a new courthouse. The Iowa firm submitted plans for the building in four months for a fee of $2,025 (about $52,000 in 2007). The plans undoubtedly were drafted so quickly because Bell and Kent had built a quite similar courthouse a few years earlier for Berrien County in St. Joseph, Michigan. The Woodford County building was completed in 1898.

In 2001, a major 57,000 square foot addition was added to the courthouse under the direction of the architectural firm of Craig, Wright and Associates.

Bell and Kent's Berrien County Courthouse in Michigan was quite similar to the Woodford County courthouse. The Berrien County building (shown) has been razed and only photographs remain for comparison.

An Illustrated History | 157

Measuring Architectural Treasures:

Courthouses and the Historic American Buildings Survey (HABS)

The Historic American Buildings Survey (HABS) is a federal program that opened its doors for business in December 1933. It was one of President Roosevelt's New Deal efforts to push back unemployment during the darkest days of America's Great Depression. In simplest terms it was a plan to give work to out-of-work architects and draftsmen. Their job would be to travel the country to record and measure old, endangered, historic buildings that were rapidly being destroyed or falling into decay.

National Park Service Director Charles E. Peterson was the program's mastermind. He had long been disturbed by the loss of historically significant structures around the USA. He hit upon the idea of providing government work to a thousand unemployed architects and draftsmen as a way to help them provide for their families and at the same time collect measurements, drawings, and histories of historic buildings.

Survey researchers often included photos as well as detailed drawings of buildings. This HABS photo of Macon County's first courthouse is a typical example. (Library of Congress)

Peterson's initial 1933 survey lasted only ten weeks. But a lot was accomplished in that short period of time. Dozens of America's antique and rapidly disappearing older buildings were measured, photographed, and documented, but perhaps more importantly, he proved the feasibility of his scheme.

Fortunately, the program has been continued in the years since. HABS is now used as a training tool for student architects and engineers and the accumulated data is an invaluable source of information for preservationists and historians. The survey is now administered through a cooperative agreement between the Park Service and the Library of Congress, and it receives support from the private sector. The survey contains more than 350,000 measured drawings, large-format photographs, and written histories for more than 35,000 historic structures and sites dating from Pre-Columbian times to the twentieth century.

Buildings with association to historic events and structures that are representative of important architectural styles continue to disappear at an alarming rate. Old buildings that had outlived their usefulness for one reason or another have always been in danger of destruction from fire or decay, but, with the unceasing sprawl of urban America, these significant structures are fading faster than ever from the landscape due to radical remodeling and, ever more frequently from demolition, impelled by cries to clear the way for urban renewal and other land development ventures.

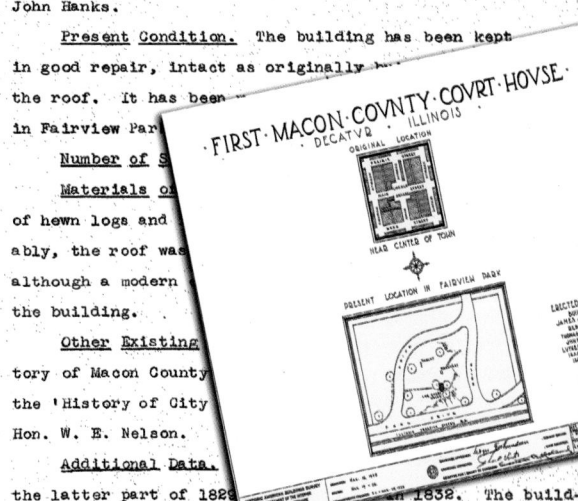

Right Top: The measured drawings show not only the dimensions of the building but indicate the addition of a new door and other changes.

Right Bottom: A HABS report on Macon County's first courthouse provides basic information about the building.

Peterson's plan was conceived hastily in the shadow of the depression but it was carried out in a systematic and professional manner, yielding lasting results.

Peterson was also pragmatic and noted in his proposal that buildings and engineering structures are large objects not easily maintained or preserved once they have outlived their functional or economic usefulness. Documentation becomes an alternative means of preservation when demolition is inevitable. Documentation is also a primary tool for the stewardship of historic structures, whether for day-to-day care or as protection from catastrophic loss.

HABS includes documentation on many different building types. The list includes public buildings, churches, residences, bridges, forts, barns, mills, shops, rural outbuildings, movie theaters, and virtually any other kind of structure that caught the attention of the survey teams and their supervisors around the country.

Sadly, not every courthouse was documented and some have been lost over time without documentation, but historians can be thankful for the ones so recorded.

The information collected on Macon County's first county courthouse shown here is representative of the work done by the survey teams during the 1930s.

The measured drawings, submitted to the National Park Service office in Washington in May 1936 were accompanied by several black and white photos of the old structure and a brief history of the building. The report includes historical notes such as the fact that Abraham Lincoln attended court in this building in 1837, only a year after he became a lawyer.

An Illustrated History | 159

About The Author

Dennis Weiser is a photojournalist who specializes in projects that combine photography of significant architecture and histories of local personalities and places. This is his second book devoted to courthouses. In 2007, he authored *Missouri Courthouses: Building Memories on the Square*. His award-winning paintings, graphic art, and photography have been exhibited at galleries and art museums throughout Missouri. He is a graduate of the University of Missouri School of Journalism, Columbia, Missouri, and holds a graduate degree from Lindenwood University at St. Charles, Missouri. His home is at Jefferson City, Missouri.

KNOX CO. COURT HOUSE,